Writing in Rhythm: Spoken Word Poetry in
Urban Classrooms
MAISHA T. FISHER

Reading the Media: Media Literacy in High School
English
RENEE HOBBS

teaching**media**literacy.com: A Web-Linked Guide to
Resources and Activities
RICHARD BEACH

What Was It Like? Teaching History and Culture
Through Young Adult Literature
LINDA J. RICE

Once Upon a Fact: Helping Children Write Nonfiction
CAROL BRENNAN JENKINS & ALICE EARLE

Research on Composition: Multiple Perspectives on
Two Decades of Change
PETER SMAGORINSKY, ED.

Critical Literacy/Critical Teaching: Tools for Preparing
Responsive Literacy Teachers
CHERYL DOZIER, PETER JOHNSTON, &
REBECCA ROGERS

The Vocabulary Book: Learning and Instruction
MICHAEL F. GRAVES

Building on Strength: Language and Literacy in Latino
Families and Communities
ANA CELIA ZENTELLA, ED.

Powerful Magic: Learning from Children's Responses
to Fantasy Literature
NINA MIKKELSEN

On the Case: Approaches to Language and Literacy
Research (An NCRLL Volume)*
ANNE HAAS DYSON & CELIA GENISHI

New Literacies in Action: Teaching and Learning in
Multiple Media
WILLIAM KIST

On Qualitative Inquiry: Approaches to Language and
Literacy Research (An NCRLL Volume)*
GEORGE KAMBERELIS &
GREG DIMITRIADIS

Teaching English Today: Advocating Change in the
Secondary Curriculum
BARRIE R.C. BARRELL, ROBERTA F. HAMMETT,
JOHN S. MAYHER, & GORDON M. PRADL, EDS.

Bridging the Literacy Achievement Gap, 4–12
DOROTHY S. STRICKLAND &
DONNA ALVERMANN, EDS.

Crossing the Digital Divide: Race, Writing, and
Technology in the Classroom
BARBARA MONROE

Out of this World: Why Literature Matters to Girls
HOLLY VIRGINIA BLACKFORD

Critical Passages: Teaching the Transition to College
Composition
KRISTIN DOMBEK & SCOTT HERNDON

Making Race Visible: Literary Research for Cultural
Understanding
STUART GREENE & DAWN ABT-PERKINS, EDS.

The Child as Critic: Developing Literacy through
Literature, K–8, Fourth Edition
GLENNA SLOAN

Room for Talk: Teaching and Learning in a
Multilingual Kindergarten
REBEKAH FASSLER

Give Them Poetry! A Guide for Sharing Poetry with
Children K–8
GLENNA SLOAN

The Brothers and Sisters Learn to Write: Popular
Literacies in Childhood and School Cultures
ANNE HAAS DYSON

"Just Playing the Part": Engaging Adolescents in
Drama and Literacy
CHRISTOPHER WORTHMAN

The Testing Trap: How State Writing Assessments
Control Learning
GEORGE HILLOCKS, JR.

The Administration and Supervision of Reading
Programs, Third Edition
SHELLEY B. WEPNER, DOROTHY S. STRICKLAND, &
JOAN T. FEELEY, EDS.

School's Out! Bridging Out-of-School Literacies with
Classroom Practice
GLYNDA HULL &
KATHERINE SCHULTZ, EDS.

Reading Lives: Working-Class Children and Literacy
Learning
DEBORAH HICKS

Inquiry Into Meaning: An Investigation of Learning to
Read, Revised Edition
EDWARD CHITTENDEN & TERRY SALINGER, WITH
ANNE M. BUSSIS

"Why Don't They Learn English?" Separating Fact
from Fallacy in the U.S. Language Debate
LUCY TSE

Conversational Borderlands: Language and Identity in
an Alternative Urban High School
BETSY RYMES

Inquiry-Based English Instruction
RICHARD BEACH & JAMIE MYERS

* Volumes with an asterisk following the title are a part of the NCRLL set: Approaches to Language and Literacy
Research, edited by JoBeth Allen and Donna Alvermann.

(Continued)

Writing in Rhythm

Spoken Word Poetry in Urban Classrooms

MAISHA T. FISHER

FOREWORD BY ANNE HAAS DYSON

TEACHERS
COLLEGE
PRESS

Teachers College, Columbia University
New York and London

Published by Teachers College Press, 1234 Amsterdam Avenue, New York, NY
10027

Library of Congress Cataloging-in-Publication Data

Fisher, Maisha T.
   Writing in rhythm : spoken word poetry in urban classrooms / Maisha T. Fisher.
     p. cm. – (Language and literacy series)
   Includes bibliographical references and index.
   ISBN 978-0-8077-4770-4 (pbk. : alk. paper)
   ISBN 978-0-8077-4771-1 (cloth : alk. paper)
     1. Poetry–Study and teaching (Secondary school)–New York (State)–
New York. I. Title.
   LB1631.F57 2007
   428.0071'2–dc22   2006101405

ISBN-13: 978-0-8077-4770-4 (paper)
ISBN-13: 978-0-8077-4771-1 (cloth)

Printed on acid-free paper
Manufactured in the United States of America

14   13   12   11   10   09   08   07   8 7 6 5 4 3 2 1

In loving memory of my mother
CHERYL A. FISHER
1951–1997

For the past, present, and future lives of
my sister-daughters and brother-sons of the Power Writers.

Thank you for teaching me how to sing.

Contents

Foreword

I blow a "C" with my harmonica. . . . "Ready to sing out your poems?" I ask
my choir. "Uno . . . dos . . . and three!"
　　　　　　　—"Juanito" in *The Upside Down Boy* (Herrera, 2000, p. 31)

Juan Felipe Herrera's picture book *The Upside Down Boy* is dedicated to his
third-grade teacher, who "first inspired me to be a singer of words, and, most
of all, a believer in my own voice" (2000, p. 32). Herrera himself once felt
upside-down, unable to find his footing in the rhythms of school life, just
like his fictionalized Juanito. Through the arts, Juanito's teacher helped him
infuse his own life rhythms into the classroom beat. Especially through the
music- and image-making power of poetry, Juanito found himself standing
tall, grounded in his new space, even as his letters poured, tumbled, crashed,
and danced on his paper. Later those letters were sung out by him in the
company of his class. "Uno, dos, and three!"

　　In this book, Maisha Fisher invites us to pull up a chair and listen in as
young people, adolescents in a New York City high school, insert their own
rhythms into school life. Guided especially by their "Power Writing" teacher
Joe, they learned to craft their feelings and reflections, their ways of talking
back to an unfair world, through spoken word poetry. Pearl and her symphony of haikus about a dreamed-of love, Karina's blues about a young life
lost, Eli's talk-back-to-power with a beat—all are examples of young people
crafting their upside-down feelings and, at times, looking critically at a topsy-
turvy world with its values askew.

　　Given the educational times, I imagine now that some potential readers,
interested in the literacy of "at-risk" adolescents, might be wondering if they
should follow Maisha Fisher into this Power Writing class. Surely spoken
word poetry is not what kids need in an urban school serving neighborhoods
in hard times. What about "skills"?!

　　But this book is not a simple celebration of student voices. It is an ethnographic account of the teaching and learning processes through which lived
(or longed-for) experience was disciplined into verbal rhythms. In this process there was a need for and attention to vocabulary that names or evokes

slippery feelings, to discursive genres that guide textual crafting, and to judicious use of what Joe called the "lush gumbo" of language (including "Bronxonics"). Moreover, the young people featured herein (like Juanito) did not do their singing alone. Their class was a kind of "home," one in which they had to learn to "feed" one another through appreciative but analytic responses to their work. Of course there were moments of teacher frustration, of kids gone silly, of disappointment. But engulfing all in the Power Writing experience was exactly what the "upside-down boy" wanted—a sense of being connected and respected, of being somebody who should be taken seriously.

Connection, respect—these are not words to be found on the public agenda these days, at least not in the classrooms I know best, those for the youngest of schoolchildren, like Juanito. There, the goal is to become a "correct" speaker and writer, not a sophisticated code-switcher, not a player with languages' varied rhythms and their reverberations of identity and tradition. This narrowness, this setting of school apart from their neighborhoods, separates children from all that grounds them and thus makes them "right-side-up." In Power Writing, though, the voices of students' everyday lives were the experiential source of inspiration, the situated stuff of critical reflection, the raw material for crafting by young poets in formation . . . as you will soon see. Maisha is waiting to take you into Joe's Power Writing class and to introduce you to the young poets. No subway token required. Just turn the page. Ready? "Uno . . . dos . . . and three!"

—Anne Haas Dyson

Acknowledgments

My greatest acknowledgment begins with the Power Writing family. I am humbled by the intellect, courage, and collective determination of these powerful young people. These poets and writers have transformed the way I walk in this world; their songs and stories give me hope and fuel my commitment to urban youth in the United States and abroad. I accept all responsibility for the way their songs and stories are presented in this text.

Joseph Ubiles was not only a "soul model" for the Power Writers; he was a soul model for me as well. Joseph, or "Papa Joe," not only allowed me to join him in his teaching journey; he also gave me reading assignments, asked difficult questions, and encouraged me to write. Shadowing Joe was like going through a teacher preparation program for a second time. He was my cooperating teacher, my New York City tour guide/historian, and now my dear friend.

Amy Sultan, Ed Sturmer, and Sammy Sturmer provided a home-away-from-home in New York City as I continued to work with the Power Writers. Their sacrifices, especially Sammy's, who always gave up his room for me, were above and beyond the call of duty. Roland Legardi-Laura continuously opened his home as a site for interviews and to all of our students, friends, and colleagues. Joe, Amy, and Roland are truly my teaching soul mates.

My postdoctoral research fellowship at Teachers College, Columbia University in Anthropology and Education provided support during this research project. I wish to acknowledge Maria Torres-Guzmán, who thought I might be interested in a "little poetry group" in the Bronx. Maria introduced me to the principal at University Heights High School, Dr. Brenda Bravo, who introduced me to Joseph Ubiles, and the rest is the future. I wish to acknowledge all of the students, support staff, and teachers at University Heights for always being gracious and welcoming. I would like to especially recognize Lillian Martinez, who is one of the most amazing school counselors I have ever seen in action.

Several people saw me through the writing journey. Ratima Guest Smith and Patrice Campbell listened to many of these ideas throughout the writing process. I am indebted to JoBeth Allen for reading chapter drafts and inviting me to share the work with her students at the University of Georgia, Athens.

JoBeth graciously invited me on a writing retreat that propelled the manuscript forward. I wish to give many thanks to Andrea Lunsford for reading and giving critical feedback to early drafts of some of the chapters. I am appreciative of my colleagues in the Division of Educational Studies at Emory University who provided a supportive environment while I was working on this manuscript. I am also grateful for the valuable feedback I received from graduate students Jill Ford, Keisha Green, Susan Hughes, and Isaac Wolf in my fall 2006 doctoral seminar. Last, but certainly not least, Valerie Kinloch, my writing partner and cheerleader, was with me during the inception of this study and in the final editing stages. Valerie offered stimulating feedback to this manuscript throughout the process.

I wish to acknowledge Carol Collins, my editor at Teachers College Press, who believed in this work and who was a joy to work with throughout the process.

My father, Dr. James A. Fisher, has supported my scholarly pursuits from the beginning. (Dad, I still remember when we were buzzing past each other in the kitchen and you stopped to say how much you supported the idea of my attending graduate school full-time.) My father and my mother, Cheryl A. Fisher, helped plant the seeds of all of my work as I witnessed their tireless commitment to education in school and in out-of-school contexts.

Damany Fisher, my brother and a doctoral candidate in the history department at the University of California, Berkeley, has been my intellectual inspiration throughout this project. I am grateful for his encouragement to consider the work of urban sociologists for this study. I am also grateful that he made himself available at any hour of the night (or morning) so I could talk through my ideas.

Last but certainly not least, I wish to thank Marlon K. Nichols for his patience and unwavering commitment to see me through the completion of this book project.

CHAPTER ONE

Learning to Sing:
The Emergence of a
New Literate and Literary

I thought that maybe if I paid more attention to the sound of words I would be able to write better. And I tried to listen more and more closely to the syllables and the vowels and everything I could possibly notice about words.

I began to think about words as a kind of music. (Jordan, 2000, pp. 48–49)

I want you to hear your music in your mind when you write and in your body when you are reading. (Joe, Power Writing Teacher, 2004)

Confession: Prior to this project, the most I knew about the Bronx was that it was one of the earliest sites for hip hop music and culture and the borough that housed the famous Yankee Stadium. I moved to New York City for a postdoctoral research fellowship, hoping to find classroom teachers who adapted out-of-school literacy practices such as spoken word poetry in the teaching of writing, reading, and speaking. One of my colleagues at Teachers College, Maria Torres-Guzmán, told me about a "little poetry group" at University Heights High School (UHHS) located in the Bronx and put me in touch with the principal, who was her old friend.

I called the school ahead of time to get directions and still got lost. I took an M60 bus down 125th Street to 5th Avenue, caught the 4 train to Burnside Avenue and was later reprimanded by students for taking the "long way" ("Why didn't you take the B or D and transfer to the 4 at Yankee Stadium???"). Once I got off the train, I found myself in a different world from my uptown (and quickly becoming gentrified) neighborhood in Harlem. Unisex salons boasting the ability to do "all types of hair," Carnicerías Hispañas, gray-haired men on the sidewalk enticing women to look at the produce in their markets, and signs for "affordable" calling cards to everywhere from the Dominican Republic to Ghana were just some of the gems in this community. Most of all I remember the music: pulsating beats of "Spanish Reggae" spilling out of cars, hip hop music floating out of apartment windows, and lyrics lingering overhead. When I approached someone whom I believed looked like me (brown skin and thick, dark hair) to ask for directions to the school, she began speaking a quick-paced Spanish that left me tongue-tied. At first she seemed confused by my inarticulate response but finally she smiled knowingly. Without another word, she grabbed my arm and gently nudged me in the right direction.

By the time I reached University Heights High School, I was hot, disappointed in my failure to show off my 8 years of studying Spanish, and feeling overdressed in my attempt to make a good impression. However, I made it to school in time for the first staff meeting, where I met Joe, "the poetry teacher." I shadowed him for the rest of the day. Joe may have been teaching in a room without windows, but his compassion forged a view many could no longer afford in New York City. His warmth and generosity made it easy to breathe. Joe's words planted seeds in timeless gardens and an otherwise hot and stuffy room became as transformative as the New York City Botanical Gardens, a place where he would eventually take his student poets. In his music appreciation class, Joe made Thelonious Monk as relevant as Tupac and Ma Rainey, as omnipresent as Mary J. Blige. After class, Joe leaned over and said, "You really have to visit my Power Writers."

During my visits to Joe's Power Writing class, I consistently noted the way Joe fluidly integrated music metaphors while teaching reading, writing and speaking. Joe would tell students, "You have to sing your piece" or "Out with it—like a singer," and this would help the most hesitant speaker begin to project his or her voice. In order to understand what it meant to "sing" in Joe's class, I began with his Power Writers. Dani explained to me, "To sing your piece is to make your piece flow. Let it spill into your audience's ears like Patti LaBelle when Motown was still Motown."

Joe's musical metaphors, or what I began to refer to affectionately as "Joe-isms," evolved from his own passion for music. It was not uncommon for Joe to compare student writing to the purpose of blues singers. Referring to the Power Writing class as a "suffering zone" because of the often complicated lives from which his students emerged as "singers," Joe understood reading, writing and speaking to be political for his students and literacy as a vehicle for enacting power over their lives and futures: "You have to be more singer-like. Your piece is a blues, and the blues is magical. Remember, the function [of the blues] is not to make you sad but to help you overcome sadness."

Forging relationships between music and student writing was a pedagogical strategy Joe employed to remind students continuously of their purpose and responsibility in Power Writing. This elective literacy class for ninth through twelfth graders, with a focus on spoken word poetry, met Monday after school and Friday mornings and was co-taught with Roland and Amy, who you will meet in Chapter 2. In addition to Mondays and Fridays, many students volunteered to meet on Saturdays and during vacations because of their enduring commitment to the group, to Joe, and to themselves. Power Writing was more than a class. It was a job, a sacred space, a home, a functional—or sometimes "dysfunctional," as one student wrote in a poem—family. Power Writing, Joe emphasized, was also an "open mic" for the "truth": "In this house, we are trying to dream ourselves a world, and we are trying to record that in the script of the English language. Your job always in here is to tell the truth."

Truth in the context of the Power Writing "house" was multiple and often shared. Power Writing was one of the most integrated chosen spaces on campus. Students wrote from the perspectives of being African American, Dominican, Puerto Rican, Colombian, El Salvadoran, West Indian, and "White," or a combination of two or more of the above. Referring to the Power Writers as "the real United Nations" in one of his own poems, Joe openly discouraged "tribalism" among his student poets and explained that, although he is a self-described Black/Puerto Rican, he was also part of a generation that focused on the shared African ancestry of African Americans, West Indians, and Latinos. In fact, Joe looked like he could be the father of any one of the Power Writers, and most students explained to me that he had become their "father figure" through the seminar. Another shared truth was the Power Writers' lives and experiences growing up in the Bronx. Students sometimes wrote of the pervasive poverty and violence on their "blocks." However, students did not romanticize these cycles; they were angry that they had to live in these conditions, and they wanted to protect their younger siblings and themselves from cycles of untimely deaths, poverty, and the temptation to surrender to it all. Power Writers were students, but in many ways they were also teachers who were forthcoming and vulnerable. Joe was the "master teacher," yet he often retreated into the background in order to invite his students to shine by openly expressing their music through words; he was an "Art Blakey" of literacy.[1]

Thus, the title of this book, *Writing in Rhythm,* is not only a reference to the way Joe helped his Power Writers begin to understand words and the writing process as a "kind of music." The term also refers to how students and teachers in the Power Writing seminar cocreated traditions around words, sounds, and power through their poetry. The aim of this book is to explore how a community of young writers with the guidance of attentive and interested adults (re)defined literacy and what it meant to be literate using the medium of spoken word poetry. When Joe explained to the Power Writers, "I want to hear your music in your mind when you write," he acknowledged the individual rhythms or the processes students brought to their writing. When Joe further emphasized the importance of hearing the music "in your body when you are reading," he underscored his trust in students' ability to make decisions about their delivery and style. In this book I offer portraits of how literate traditions were cocreated in a writing seminar during one school year.

At the beginning of this project, I wanted to know how teachers were integrating out-of-school literacy practices, such as spoken word poetry, in school contexts. My interests evolved from a previous study I conducted of spoken word poetry venues and author events in Black bookstores in Northern California (Fisher, 2003a; 2003b; 2004; 2006a). I thought if I could understand the salient characteristics of "chosen" literacy spaces that fostered participation, then I could somehow use this knowledge to inform the way English language arts classroom communities are conceptualized. Power Writing pedagogy employed an "open mic" ideology immersed in the tradition that people should have a forum where they can exchange ideas. Through the act of reciprocity, the Power Writers and their teachers built a literocracy, a space in which each participant had an opportunity to access both written and spoken words while speaking his or her own truth. Elsewhere, I have defined *literocracy* as "an intersection of literacy and democracy" that "blurs boundaries of oral/aural and written while emphasizing that language processes exist in partnership with action in order to guide young people to develop a passion for words and language" (Fisher, 2005a, p. 92). From working with the Power Writers I also learned that a literocracy helps students develop a sense of purpose around reading, writing, and speaking (Fisher, 2005b, 2006b). The theoretical underpinnings in a literocracy are grounded in understanding literacy as critical (Freire & Macedo, 1987; Shor, 1992), as a social practice (Heath, 1983; Scribner & Cole, 1981; Street, 1984,

---

1. Jazz drummer and composer Art Blakey mentored countless jazz musicians throughout his career as the leader of a rotating collective of musicians known as The Jazz Messengers. I discuss this connection in greater detail in Chapter 7.

1993, 2005), and as Democratic Engagement (Kinloch, 2005a). Joe often described his teaching as "Freirian" in nature and cited Freire in his reflective essay titled "To Teach Power Writing": "Power Writing has its origins in the very powerful idea of Paulo Freire that education is always an act of 'intervention in the world.' . . . In Power Writing we value the idea of teachers as learners and learners as teachers" (Ubiles, 2004, p. 18).

In conceptualizing *literocracy*, literacy is an act of reciprocity; you pass on what you know, and all participants have an opportunity to cultivate their mind with the skills they bring. In this book I sought to unpack how teachers such as Joe used spoken word poetry as a tool to

- Introduce students to a writing workshop format or the "read and feed" process
- Address the politics of "Bronxonics" and "Standard American English"
- Introduce new vocabulary by "fishing for" or "catching" words
- Encourage students to become modern blues writers or to tell their individual and shared truths through original poetry and prose
- Aspire to push beyond "ascribed lives"

SPOKEN WORD ACTIVISM AND THE "NU YOR ROCK"

Defining poetry as "a revolt, a scream in the night, an emancipation of old ways of thinking," Kelley (2002) demonstrates the critical role that poetry has played in activism and struggle. Kelley's work provides a framework for understanding Joe's purpose for the Power Writers: "In the poetics of struggle and lived experiences, in the utterances of ordinary folks, in the cultural products of social movements, in the reflections of activists, we discover the many different cognitive maps of the future, of the world not yet born" (p. 9).

I would argue that Power Writing is an example of one of the "cognitive maps of the future"; in this class the word *literacy* flew high like a flag celebrating one's love for his or her country. At other times literacy resembled a multicolored kite anchored by a spool of thread held by many hands. Joe's orientation toward his teaching and his students was inextricably linked to his experiences while coming of age as a poet and activist. By creating an open mic atmosphere in his classroom (in this case, the "read and feed" process discussed extensively in Chapter 3), Joe drew from the traditions of out-of-school literacy spaces, like the Nuyorican Poets Café, to demonstrate multiple ways of being literate. Therefore, when Joe told his Power Writers, "I want you to be literate in as many ways as possible," the students saw him model the literate behaviors he expected them to develop. Joe wrote and performed his work alongside student poets. As a certified tour guide of New York City and a social historian, Joe looked for opportunities to merge history and language arts. When Joe wrote his poem, "Nuyorican Poets Café, East 3rd Street, Atlantis," for the Power Writers, he contextualized the café's legacy in the poetry community while carving out space for them to be a part of poetry's future:

> East of the sun
> And west of the moon
> At the Nu Yor Rock
> Where the clock never stops
> Between Avante Gardes and Hip Hop
> On the block
> Where
> Slugs once wuz
> Where
> Lee Morgan died
> Inside
> Where gunshots like sidewinders
> Cud kill a musician but not the music
> Where we be
> Avenue C
> Where the great Sun Ra played
> Evening to morning intergalactic blue/jazzness
> Where wives were discovered
> And discarded
> Among empty bottles of Remy Martin
> And plugs of black gum opium
> Where
> The stairwells and rooftops once flowered
> With glass syringes
> And burnt bottle caps
> And bloody cotton
> Where the cooker became both icon and emblem
> Of our demise
> And our distraction
>
> Peace Gods
> The Nuyoricans live
> The Blacks live
> The poor assed white boys live
> Where the Nuyorican Poets Café lives
> Where
> Truth sprouts

From Mama's rice and beans
Collard greens
Work torn knees
Where a harvest of pink
Yellow
Tan brown black titans is reaped and sown
Where thousand headed griots of the
Bacalao and black bean nations
Azucar
Rice and cotton nations
Stoop labor
Day labor
Factory work nations
Welfare workfare no car fare nations
No fresh air no "good" hair much despair nations
Gather as the voices of poetry
Of kingdoms yet to come
Yet all there
Platanos all
Negros all
Without reference to who used to own us
Defiant in our ignorant wisdoms and sorrowful pleasures
Where
Now is now and then is then
Where
The young are rising
Like Phoenix
Like Osiris
Like Jesus
As oracles of change
As the babaloas of new/ancient
Machete dreams of freedom
Peace
And venceremos
My people.

In his poem to his students, Joe asserted a space for the Power Writers in history by placing them "East of the sun" and "West of the moon" at this cornerstone for poetry and living arts. "Remixing" or rearranging "Nuyori-can" to the "Nu Yor Rock," Joe attempted to reflect his students' love of hip hop music while making the café as relevant to them as it was for Joe as a young poet. Joe also situated student writing between traditions in jazz music or "Avante Gardes" and hip hop music. In other words, both traditions and everything in between were branches on the same family tree anointing the Power Writers as part of a continuum of poets and writers. While not romanticizing this era, Joe acknowledged the Nuyorican Poet's Café as a site for hope and possibility, "of kingdoms yet to come," in the middle of chaos. Joe saw the Power Writers as a recent manifestation of this hope "where the young are rising . . . as oracles of change." Algarín (1994), poet and cofounder of the café, asserts the poetry that has evolved from this café and movement "has to be responsible for giving a direction, for illuminating a path" (pp. 10–11). This journey with Joe and the Power Writers is an invitation for teachers, teacher educators, and literacy researchers to follow this map and participate in the Power Writers' journey to write their life stories and use it to imagine a world they desire.

OUTLINE OF THE BOOK

In Chapter 2, I introduce the Power Writing seminar, Joe and his copilots, Amy and Roland, and of course the Power Writers themselves. In this chapter I provide a discussion of the research methods used in this study and draw specific attention to the valuable role of ethnographic video.

In Chapters 3, 4, 5, and 6, I move from an overview of the Power Writing community to the particulars of the Power Writing process. In Chapter 3 I examine the peer feedback process known as "reading and feeding," which was at the core of the Power Writing seminar. Using ethnographic descriptions, transcribed classroom discourse, and interview data from students, I demonstrate how students learned to engage one another through their writing. I also explore the tensions in trying to foster a safe space for students to share their work.

In Chapter 4 I begin with a discussion of Students' Right to Their Own Language (SRTOL) in order to show how the Power Writers confronted issues of "standard" and "nonstandard" English or "Englishes" in their writing. "Bronxonics," a term coined by Joe, encapsulated the various styles and terminology used by students in class. Here, I hope to contribute to teachers' ongoing struggles to find respectful approaches for discussing language.

In Chapter 5 I introduce the practice of "fishing for" or "catching" words. In this chapter I use classroom vignettes to demonstrate how Joe attempted to teach vocabulary in context and stage dialogue around specific vocabulary words. Like Jordan's and Joe's quotes that open this chapter, students learned to think about works as "a kind of music" by listening to sounds and syllables.

In Chapter 6 I explore the history of truth-telling and relationships between the blues epistemology, rap music, and spoken word poetry. In this chapter I focus on student poetry that follows the tradition of blues music as "embedded, necessary, and reflective" (Woods, 1998, p. 25).

In Chapter 7 I move away from the core of the Power Writing seminar and use the trajectory of one Power Writer who joined the group late in the semester in order to underscore the methods used to help students build literate identities. I also draw from data gathered in one-on-one interviews with the Power Writers for a focused discussion of the implications this study carries for both schools and communities.

CHAPTER TWO

Soul Models,
Rebel Voices, or "Who We Be"

A week after I met Joe, I was sitting in a circle with some of the "old school" Power Writers, or the first-generation poets of the seminar. When Joe asked me to introduce myself, I explained that I was a former elementary and high school teacher from California. Syesha interrupted, "Were you the kind of teacher that students loved or hated?" That was it—either I was "loved" or "hated" as a teacher; Syesha did not see any middle ground. I replied, "I'd like to think I was the kind of teacher that my students loved."

Syesha demanded "How do I know that? You're probably lying." I surrendered by tell-
ing her, "So I guess you will have to get to know me for yourself." Syesha insisted that I
had to write when they wrote. Ramon quizzed me on my hip hop knowledge; he wanted
to know if I listened to conscious hip hop or "the stuff they play on the radio." When he
found out that I knew about his favorite emcee, Immortal Technique, he gave me props
and let me off the hook. Pearl and Dani asked me if I grew up in the "ghetto" or a "rich
neighborhood." When I said that my life was somewhere in between, they said "Oh–
you're bourghetto" (a hybrid of the bourgeoisie and working class), and Pearl further
explained, "My sister acts like you–she sounds like a Valley Girl and everything."

Joe never interrupted this interrogation, although I must admit that I waited for him
to come to my rescue. I was in the Power Writers' space, where they cocreated and defined
what it meant to be in the circle. In my heart I knew that Syesha, Ramon, Pearl, and
Dani were justified in their suspicion of a stranger with a "funny accent" showing up in
their sacred space. During the first of what would be many train rides together, Joe care-
fully explained, "At the end of the day, I need for you as a young brown person to show
my other young brown people that they have many options in their lives."

In her autobiography, titled *Soldier: A Poet's Childhood* (2000), poet and activist June Jordan described her father's love for beautiful things and his desire
to capture them on film. Jordan recalled watching her father painstakingly
arrange a Chinese vase and "truly beautiful" pieces of fruit to photograph.
As he arranged and rearranged these items, Jordan noted, "it did seem to
me that just being chosen made you beautiful" (p. 128). Joe sometimes chose
Power Writers, and at other times the Power Writers chose Joe. During individual interviews, students shared with me that Joe had invited them to
the Power Writing seminar after he witnessed them in heated debates with
teachers or other students in the hallways of UHHS. He would challenge
them to put their passion and energy on paper. Joe would also ask students
who sat quietly–or not so quietly–in the back of his other classes to join the
Power Writing community where he could give them more support outside
of class. Joe had taught just about everything, including English, astronomy,
history, and music appreciation. Many of the Power Writers were former
members of his advisory, or "family group," one of the small homerooms
that alternative high schools like UHHS instituted in order to help students
develop personal relationships with at least one teacher. Some Power Writers were invited to class by peers who were either friends or classmates.
Lillian, the school counselor and Power Writing advocate, often encouraged
students to participate as well. Regardless of how students came to Power
Writing, it was the act of being "chosen" by an attentive, open-minded adult
or a peer who had experienced the feeling of being cherished that created
a sense of beauty in this seminar. During Power Writing, Joe told students
who transformed over time, "I claim you." This coronation was taken very
seriously.

THE BRONX DIASPORA

Who are the Power Writers and who are the teachers/soul models who have committed themselves to these young people? One book cannot do justice to their words, sound, and power, nor can a chart (see Appendix A for information about the students). At the time of my study, UHHS had 367 ninth- through twelfth-grade students: 56.9% "Hispanic," 39.9% "Black," with "Asian" and "White" making up the remaining population. "Hispanic" largely included Dominican and Puerto Rican students in addition to those of Central American heritage. "Black" referred to African American, West Indian, and African immigrants, with the latter two having a range of meanings as well. Although the Power Writing class was arguably one of the most integrated chosen spaces on campus, students were welcome to celebrate their heritage. In spite of the fact that the group defied categories, one description of the Power Writers resonated with me, and I continued to revisit it throughout this study. On a snowy Tuesday night in February, 22 Power Writers (with representatives from their families or circle of friends) traveled from their Bronx neighborhoods to Roland's loft in the East Village to participate in a reading being held in their honor. Roland emceed the reading, explaining to the audience that the night had been organized to "celebrate the work, discipline, perseverance, and pure genius" of the Power Writers' "Rebel Voices":

> And these kids are rebels in two ways. Some of them are political rebels. They're all rebels because what they have all done is rebel against the little slot, the little block in the pyramid that society has chosen for them. And they have chosen to rebel in the deepest, most profound way with their power, with their literacy, and this Power Writing workshop that we have is about helping them discover that. In fact it has been a discovery for all of us.

Roland's depiction of the Power Writers, embedded in their "Rebel Voices," could not have been more accurate. Through writing and performing, Power Writers refused to live in a "little slot" or a "little block." Interaction with so many different people in their class, or what Joe referred to as "the Bronx Diaspora," and field trips to venues throughout New York City were part of the discovery process for students and co-teachers.

That same night, Roland introduced Joe to the audience. Joe was humble when asked about his role with the Power Writers. Roland coined the term *soul model* when he introduced Joe at this public reading:

> ROLAND: We've got Joe with us here—Joe has been my teacher this last year and a half. If there is a term a *master teacher*, it would be coined for Joe.

He's found a way not just for these kids to learn, but he is a role model and a soul model. And he is such an extraordinary example of what dedication can be. If the whole school system had 10 Joes, it would be improved. If it had 20 Joes, we'd be in another universe.

SYESHA (shouting out from the audience): If we had 50 Joes we'd have to pay to get in the school!

ROLAND: That's right!

Syesha perceived a school full of "Joes" as one that would be inaccessible to public school students. "Fifty Joes," in Syesha's mind, was the equivalent of paying tuition. Joe saw the Power Writers in many different ways, but ultimately he considered his class to be a family:

> The classroom has elements of the traditional family; there is trust involved. My students' prior knowledge is profoundly respected by me and at some level exalted. This is not an attempt to colonize them. It is an attempt to extend on their natural learning capacity; there is nothing more essentially human than the act of learning and the act of teaching. A class like Power Writing should be available to all for them.

Joe generously shared his role as a "soul model" with Amy and Roland. Amy, an executive director of a nonprofit organization called Early Stages that provided free theater tickets to students in New York City public schools, discovered Joe during her visits to UHHS and immediately wanted to participate and find opportunities to fund class activities. Amy introduced Joe to Roland, who was an artist-in-residence with Early Stages and a board member for the Nuyorican Poets Café. Roland, a poet and documentary filmmaker, shared Joe's ideology about the power of literacy. Joe taught on Monday afternoons and co-taught with Roland and Amy on Friday mornings. The catalyst for these introductions was Lillian, a parent volunteer turned school counselor. At some point, all of Lillian's three sons participated in Power Writing, even when they were not students at UHHS. Although she did not attend all of the classes, Lillian was a card-carrying member of the Power Writers and held the affection of the students. Many other adults came in and out of the space to show their quiet support, including the principal and the College Now advisor. When I began to observe the Power Writers in the fall of 2003, I had the audacity to think I would be a visitor. Over time, however, I shed the title of "guest" and was recruited as a co-teacher. We noted that our teaching team was a "United Nations" of sorts: Roland is Italian, Amy is Jewish, and I am Black. We never attended any training together—our common ground was our love for young people and our desire to see the Power Writers read, write, and speak for a variety of purposes.

A soul model—as opposed to a role model—consistently grows with his or her students while making the process as visible as possible. A soul model has a wealth of life experiences from which he or she can draw, and is constantly challenging his or her own thinking about the world. A soul model is also a practitioner of the craft: He or she does not merely assign reading and writing, he or she is a reader and writer.

While Joe remained the primary teacher, students witnessed a range of personalities, styles, and ways of living through all of us. When I met Joe, he had been teaching at UHHS for approximately five years; he carried a "temporary" teaching certification that was renewed annually. Roland was working on a documentary, critiquing the "dumbing down" of education inspired by the work of his former middle-school teacher and author John Gatto. Amy had a rich background in grant writing and working for non-profits; her grant-writing skills made it possible to publish the *Rebel Voices from the Heights Anthology* and to support Saturday classes. Although I carried multiple-subject and single-subject teaching credentials in English from the state of California, I considered myself a student teacher working under these three gifted educators.

One of our "shared truths" was that we wanted the Power Writers to read, write, and speak about the world they believed they should have. Roland footnoted this ideal by saying, "the more you can express about yourself and the world around you, the more powerful you can become." It is important to note that our efforts to encourage the Power Writers to read, write, and speak about subjects that impacted their lives did not overshadow our consistent efforts to teach skills such as vocabulary, literary devices, and the Language of Wider Communication (LWC). Christensen (2000) underscores this point with suggestions for building a "community" out of "chaos": "I want to be clear: Bringing student issues into the room does not mean giving up teaching the core ideas and skills of the class; it means using the energy of their connections to drive us through the content" (p. 5).

All too often there is an assumption in the education community that promoting student self-awareness through writing and performance means that students are not acquiring the skills they need for "academic literacy." In the 21st century, the traditional English teacher has to be so much more; he or she also has to be a healer. This is especially true in urban public schools. Rhythm and fluidity with words and language can no longer be a luxury; it is imperative that students have access to the "standard" and more. Approaching students as if they had prior knowledge and possibly "exalting" that knowledge was a lesson that Amy, Roland, and I learned well from Joe. He looked beyond clothing, hairstyles, attempts to posture, and at times some choice words from the students, to help them uncover their gifts using the medium of literacy.

"NEW YORK CITY BELONGS TO YOU": MULTIPLE SITES/SIGHTS

Power Writing had multiple venues. Joe's small Monday afternoon classes were held in his shared classroom at UHHS, the larger Friday morning classes were held in a classroom that belonged to Bronx Community College (BCC), and Saturday classes were held primarily at Roland's loft in the East Village, but the class also met at various venues throughout the city. When class was held in Joe's shared classroom at UHHS, students would arrange their desks in a circle, semicircle, or other shapes that allowed them to see each other. Joe purposefully sat among the students in order to maintain eye contact and to demonstrate that he was a part of the circle. The Friday room had large tables pushed together in the middle with chairs lining the perimeter. The windows in this room were always open regardless of the season, and the rustling of plastic vertical blinds provided a predictable soundtrack. The tall ceilings and cement floors invited echoes, and sounds reverberated throughout the room and down the hallway. One of the advantages of arriving at Friday morning classes early was getting prime seating around the table. Once seating around the table was full, students sat either on stools or on the large windowsills.

Saturday attendance was high. Students looked forward to the adventure and the "Amy food" (bagels, lox, "stinky cheeses," and lots of fresh fruits and juices). We often had honorary guests, including the younger siblings, cousins, neighbors, and friends of the Power Writers. Because many of our Saturday classes took place in Roland's loft, I began to refer to them as "loft-learning." Students loved the loft space; they could engage in different activities and still be able to see and hear each other. Some students would be working on their writing in the library/office area while others were reading books on the built-in benches. Many gathered in the living room where Roland set up the microphone, while some preferred to be more isolated in one of the side rooms where there was desk space. Joe, Roland, Amy, and I could move from space to space, assisting students with their writing or listening to them practice. For many Power Writers, Roland's loft was one of the few spaces they could work on their writing without interruption. Students were invited to talk, listen to music, and move around, and then Joe and Roland would call everyone to the living room space around the microphone. They would talk about the goals or objectives for the day and do one or two rounds of read and feed.

During my study, the Power Writers also experienced the Cloisters, various places on the Upper West Side (Columbia University, Teachers College, Grant's Tomb, Riverside Church, St. John's Cathedral), the New York City Botanical Gardens (located in the Bronx), the Brooklyn Botanical Gardens, the Hamilton Grange House, Urban Word NYC Teen Slam competitions (which took place at various venues throughout New York City, including the Nuyorican Poets Café and the Apollo Theater), and the premier of *Fahrenheit 9/11*. Joe was very candid with students about their limited knowledge of New York City beyond their blocks and addressed this issue in the seminar:

> In my mind, New York City belongs to you. In my mind I never, ever, ever want to hear my sons and daughters live 100 yards from the Botanical Gardens but they ain't never been there. I'm not ashamed of you but I know why. I know why. I heard one of the New York City librarians talking, and she said, "Yeah, yeah, yeah, this is New York City where people stand with their foot on the wall outside the library but they don't go in." That's the truth. You're not supposed to know. Your lives are ascribed.

Many Power Writers lived within walking distance of the New York City Botanical Gardens but had never considered going inside. The same was true for many of the venues throughout the city. While Joe emphasized that he knew why many of the students had not gone into the Botanical Gardens, he did not let anyone shirk the responsibility of learning, trying new things, and meeting different kinds of people. Power Writers learned to do more than use the library as a rest stop; they began to take ownership of public institutions.

A NOTE ON METHODS

Worthy Witnessing

I want to be clear that I did not study UHHS; I did not formally observe other teachers, classrooms, or the Power Writers in their other classes. Since I spent a great deal of time at the school, I became familiar with members of the staff and especially teachers who believed in Joe's work with the Power Writers. It is important to note that UHHS was an alternative high school embedded in the small learning community tradition. Every student at UHHS had an advisory or family group. Lieber and Poliner (2004) assert that although advisory programs may vary from school to school, their primary goals are to help students adjust to their grade levels and foster a "sense of belonging," while establishing relationships built on respect and providing an advisor or coach so that students have at least one teacher who knows them intimately (p. 11). Joe firmly believed that the advisory model, and family groups in particular, provided high school students with a strong foundation for creating a community.

I was a participant observer in the Power Writing class on Mondays after school, Friday mornings, and Saturdays from September 2003 through June 2004. I continued to follow Joe's work with the Power Writers during the 2004–2005 and 2005–2006 school years; however, the data in this book focus on my first year. As a participant observer, I kept ethnographic field notes, videotaped sessions, and interviewed students during the second semester. Although I followed an interview protocol, the interviews became more like conversations over time. I set up formal times to interview students and continued these conversations throughout the year. Since I saw students at least three days a week, we were always expanding on ideas. Not every student was comfortable being interviewed, and I honored this, but most students asked me when they would be interviewed. One of the critical parts of each interview was asking students to define class transactions. I had my own ideas of what these "Joe-isms" meant, but it was more important to gain an understanding through the students. Later, Joe and I discussed the student definitions, and he believed that the Power Writers' interpretations of what he was saying in class helped his teaching tremendously. Interviews with Joe, Roland, and Amy were conversations in context that took place throughout the year. At the end of the spring of 2004, the four of us created our own working retreat to discuss the strengths, challenges, and future direction of the program.

During the study, I wrote an article using preliminary data that I shared with Joe. One day, when I was interviewing a student, Joe came by to "feed" me, or give me feedback on the article draft. Joe expressed that he knew what he was doing but never knew if anyone else understood what he was trying to do: "I feel valued and I feel like you witnessed things and you were a legitimate witness. You are a worthy witness. It is a witnessing."

I believe that part of being a "worthy witness" is becoming involved in the teaching and learning communities that have welcomed you as a researcher. I moved to New York City with specific questions about the intersections of out-of-school and in-school literacy practices, but the more I learned about this particular writing community, the more questions I had. I have never spent time in an urban public school that had the luxury of allowing an able-bodied person to sit quietly in the corner without making some kind of contribution. They put me to work, and I was happy to oblige. The role of a worthy witness is keeping the naming actions of the community intact to preserve the integrity of Joe's teaching voice; Joe-isms were an essential coding category. Descriptive codes for the skills Joe continuously emphasized in class included literacy/being literate, Jedi of words, singing, read and feed/reading and feeding, Bronxonics, fishing for/catching words, and truth-telling/telling the truth/Blues singing (see Appendix B for examples of Joe-isms, students' definitions, and Joe's explanations that may also appear in context elsewhere in the book).

"Let the Camera Help You":
Ethnographic Video in the Literacy Classroom

The video camera, a Sony Digital Video Camera Recorder (DCR-TRV), served multiple functions in this study, although I initially thought of it as a tool for capturing dialogue between students and teachers as well as between students and their peers. I used video footage to amplify field notes; spoken word poetry is meant to be heard and performed, and traditional field notes capture only part of the story. During the 2004–2005 academic year, I digitized the Mini DV/digital videocassettes in order to begin the coding process. The digitizing process was a learning journey graciously guided by staff members at Emory's Center for Information and Technology (ECIT). During the digitizing process, I kept what I refer to as "video field notes," which included my ethnographic notes, partial transcriptions of student talk, teacher talk, and poetry shared during the "read and feed" process. The digitizing process and video field notes aided me in the coding of class transactions, or "chapters" in class sessions. In those class sessions when the camera became inappropriate, I immediately switched it off. In her study of "visual ethnography," Pink (2001) contends, "Ethnographers should develop a self-conscious approach not only to their relationships with the video subjects but also to how both relate to the camera" (p. 78). Students signed releases to be filmed; however, every day was treated like a new day, and I constantly checked in with students about their comfort with the camera.

Joe often told the Power Writers to "let the camera help you." Joe wanted students to use the filming as an opportunity to work through their fears of public speaking and he encouraged students to see the camera as a representative of the world that was listening and watching. Joe's ultimate objective was for students to become so confident in their work that they would either forget about or stop caring about the camera. The camera became community property. Students often wanted to hold it and would pass the camera around the table. The camera was also small enough that it could be propped up in the corner of the room without being intrusive. An LCD panel allowed me and other camerapersons to be present in the room and also allowed students to review footage while rehearsing for public readings.

TRAINING THE JEDI OF WORDS: A LITERACY APPRENTICESHIP

The original *Star Wars* trilogy introduced the Jedi knight. A Jedi knight was known for his focus and unwavering commitment to training. Jedi knights were also known to have self-discipline and determination. However, the second phase of training involved an apprenticeship, with the goal of becoming a "Jedi Master." Power Writing was an apprenticeship, and Joe wanted his Power Writers to apply the same sense of urgency shown by a Jedi to their literacy skills: "I want you to become a Jedi of words." Like Jedi knights striving to become a "master," Power Writers needed tools. These tools included a journal or "book of seeds," a voice, and the capacity to listen and be open to new knowledge and travel (beyond one's block and borough). Additionally, a "Jedi of words" had to:

- Participate actively in the read and feed process;
- Understand the musicality, beauty, *and* limitations of "Bronxonics";
- Improve his or her vocabulary by "fishing" for words or "catching words";
- Tell the "truth" "always" in the blues tradition;
- Aspire beyond "ascribed lives".

Joe's objective was that each Power Writer could take ownership of his or her reading, writing, and speaking processes. However, to become a "Jedi of words," learners had to be dedicated and willing to practice. The next chapter describes the foundation of the Power Writing class: the read and feed process.

CHAPTER THREE

"I Want to Hear Your Music": The Art of Reading and Feeding

"We have class at 9:00 A.M. on Saturday morning?" I asked Joe in disbelief.

"Yeah, kid, see you there," Joe responded before asking, "Are you going to get lost again? I can draw a map for you."

Joe relentlessly teased me about my West Coast orientation. I was becoming accustomed to it. I was less concerned about getting lost than about getting up early on a Saturday. However, when I arrived to UHHS at 9:00 A.M. sharp, Alberto, Pearl, Karina and Buddha, along with Joe, Amy, and Roland, were already talking and eating. Croissants, apples, pears, and organic apple juice were available to the students. Alberto and Buddha were having a "quotation battle" on the chalkboard, both of them writing feverishly until the entire board was filled with quotes from various poets. Joe asked for everyone's attention and opened the circle, saying, "I want you to become a Jedi of language. No one will be able to speak language above you, and there will be nothing written that you don't comprehend. . . . I really want you to fly out of here every day."

Joe instructed everyone to write for 20 minutes and be "intellectually clear" about their "desire" to write. As Alberto read his poem, some students were arriving late, tiptoeing into the room, waving or blowing kisses, and sliding into empty chairs as if they had been there all the time. Alberto read: "Like a dolphin to the ocean, the pen returns to paper. It leaks its blood on the dead tree bark, and with it forms aesthetic words of adoration. For so long, any pen that has met this hand has wept songs of lamentation . . . sorry for the world and what it has become; sorry for mankind; sorry for injustice. . . . " One student who arrived late immediately jumped in and "fed" Alberto, saying, "Yo, you got skills, my man." We smiled as these two young men gave each other feedback on their own terms.

Pearl read, "I scream onto my pages knowing they can't talk back, writing to escape my world. I live in a world filled with drug dealers and crackheads/And I'd rather create a new world/Better than my own/I feel free to write and make up a world far better in comparison to my reality. . . . " Students fed her by telling her that she was "singing" the poem and that they could "really hear the rhythm."

By noon, everyone in the room had read at least one poem and received feedback from at least one of their peers and one adult. Joe closed the circle by making eye contact with everyone and saying, "Writers need a home. I really want to welcome you. I believe in the process." From that point on, whenever Joe told me we had class on Saturday, I simply responded, "I'm there."

"Reading and feeding" formed the core of Power Writing. To be literate in the art of reading and feeding, students not only had to read their original writing, but they also had to be active listeners and engage each other with detailed feedback. Everyone had to participate in the "wheel," including teachers and guests. During read and feed, Power Writers were asked to read or recite one of their poems and enlist the feedback of at least two people in the circle. If there were time constraints, readers were limited to one feeder. Providing feedback was referred to as "feeding"; this was the way every member of the community received nourishment for his or her work. Feeding was also an exercise in active listening. Students could not get enough of this process, and if time permitted, they requested a second round of read and feed (and a third, and a fourth . . .). Feeding had to be more than just affirming and complimentary; it had to be informed, critical, and specific. Joe and Roland used the read and feed process to introduce new vocabulary words, including definitions for styles of writing, in addition to coaching students with their public speaking and critical thinking. Joe also used read and feed to underscore his confidence in every student's ability to become a strong writer. Roland used read and feed to help Power Writers think about presentation and voice. Amy tailored her feeding to what she believed a particular student needed at a particular time. I used read and feed to help students see their evolution over time. Since I was reviewing field notes and video footage, I was able to articulate the growth I witnessed weekly.

Many feeders began their Power Writing careers by providing minimal feedback, such as "I liked it." In order to push students to expand their thinking, Joe or Roland might ask, "What did you like about it? Why? What words are new to you?" Because read and feed was so critical to Power Writing, the purpose of this chapter is to examine this practice using the following questions as a guide:

- What were the salient characteristics of the read and feed process? How did teachers and students create a climate for this process?
- What were the ways teachers fed students and students fed one another?
- What happened when read and feed did not go smoothly? How did teachers and students respond?

Instructions for read and feed were a work in progress, and peer feedback varied in detail and length. However, there were a few grounding principles. Students had to be "clapped in" and "clapped out," or given a round of applause to foster encouragement. Joe and Roland would often footnote one another's instructions by offering more examples or clarification. For example, Joe would begin with, "You have to be able to say why you liked the poem. If you hear something really good, we want you to apply the principle in your own writing." Roland emphasized the need for "detailed and specific critique" and would urge the Power Writers to "pick an image out of the poem that affected you." Power Writers also defined the process for themselves:

> In the beginning, nobody really knows how to feed. You know "it was good," "you liked it." It took me a while to get out of that zone. . . . I learned that being a good feeder is [more than] saying what you liked about it. I think saying an exact phrase and breaking it down. . . . I don't let anything distract me. I feed in three parts. First, [I feed] with my own experiences. . . . Secondly, I criticize—like I talk about their performance, projection that shows their ability and how their poem comes out to us; and also it's just when I feed someone, I like to take out an exact part so they know I was listening and that I understood it because that works for me. . . . I know if I break it down and show you how to do better, then you can understand I'm not being mean, but I know there's more to you. (Pearl, first-generation Power Writer)

Feeding helped individual students monitor their growth and development as writers and speakers, while also giving the collective group a chance to experience new styles, words, and approaches to writing. I was always impressed with the patience displayed during read and feed. Joe was able to focus on encouraging the students' desire to write more. Because of Joe's patience and respect for every student, the Power Writers discovered how to talk to each other about their work with honesty and passion. The breakthroughs, however, happened when students were able to feed one another and examine their own process. In this chapter, I contextualize the process using vignettes from Power Writing classes.

PEARL'S SYMPHONY

Pearl was considered one of the most skilled poets in the group by her peers. Joe introduced Pearl to haiku, and she struggled with the form. However, Joe kept pushing Pearl, believing that once she grew comfortable with the form she would "run with it." On this particular Monday, Pearl was unveiling her haikus. It was a small class that included two of the "old school" Power Writers, Pink and Joel; some "new school" Power Writers, Yari and Aleyva; and visiting Power Writers Danielle and Rob. A former student of Joe's, Rob returned to campus specifically to attend Power Writing. His sister, Robbin, was a Power Writer but was unable to attend Monday classes. Rob was a self-taught musician who learned to play piano by listening rather than reading music. Joe asked Pearl to share her "symphony" with the class and for everyone to feed her:

JOE: Pearl actually has a symphony. In how many movements? In six
    movements?
PEARL: Five. I don't have them typed.
JOE: But you have a succession of haikus. At some level repeated haikus or
    extended haikus are called Tanka, Waka, or Renga.
PEARL (reciting her poem):

> Juicy lips, soft hair
> Light skin on my open mind
> I can't seem to sleep

> Smells of your sweet scent
> Seems to be in every room
> I love to smell you

I look in your eyes
Seducing you openly
Tasting your sweet juice

In my mind you're there
In my dreams you're always there
I'm waiting for you

Playing with your hair
Afraid he hears my heart speak
He gives me a high

YARI: It's strong in the beginning but then the high just tears up my heart. I was waiting for more–a usually happy ending.
JOE: Feed her, Rob. What did she make you feel?
ROB: I don't know.
JOE: What did you hear? What music did you hear when she was reading? Did you hear any?
ROB: What do you mean?
JOE: If she was reading, what music would you play behind her?
ROB: Oh. "All My Life."
JOE: Does anyone know that song?
JOEL: K-Ci and Jo Jo?
PEARL (singing the words): *All my life, I prayed for someone like you . . .*
JOEL: I used to like it but then it got played out.
JOE: But did that serve you? Would you play that song?
PEARL (smiling widely): Yes, I would.
JOE: Okay, alright. Then that's a match.
YARI: That's a beautiful match.
JOE: Danielle?
DANIELLE: It was good.
JOE: Okay.
ALEYVA: It makes me feel what she's saying. A lot of feelings.
YARI: I feel that way sometimes.
JOE: What do you feel?
YARI: I feel that way sometimes.
JOE [addressing Pearl]: Okay. Alright. Now that's interesting. You know. See how strong [it is]?
JOEL: How could I put it? In every person I think there's sort of that love, and I feel like you portrayed it really beautifully with your haikus. Most of the time haikus are meant to be something–it really is meant to be a one-hitter quitter. But these didn't quit you in one hit. It flowed well. Even though the form wasn't meant for that. That's what I felt like it really just carries you in. It carries you like a road with hills. That's what I

felt like. There were some high parts, and then it lets you down, but not down in the sense that it gets boring, but in the sense that the excitement goes down a little. Just pay attention to detail. I felt like it was very nice.

PEARL: Thank you.

JOE: I feel like I won because you resisted haiku for so long, but today you very deliberately in a very public forum decided not only to read a very intimate thought but to use a form that you really weren't happy with in the beginning. And now I think you see the efficiency in the form. So my grievance was "cherry lips" but "juicy lips" works for me. [Laughter]

YARI: It gives it taste.

JOE: I think it's highly successful, so we need to type these. Then we'll separate them, and then we'll name then.

In a study of listening in classroom communities, Schultz (2003) defines listening as "an active, relational, and interpretive process that is focused on making meaning" (p. 8). Schultz uses this definition to distinguish between "teaching as telling" and teaching as an engaged practice in which teachers are also learners. Joe sat among his students, taking notes and, most important, listening so he could find the rhythm of the group and make informed decisions about where his voice should enter. As in Schultz's study, listening with the Power Writers included spoken and unspoken words, movement and stillness. As students thoughtfully fed Pearl around her haikus, Joe also listened as an engaged learner. This was a strategy Joe employed during read and feed, and it was true to his Freire-inspired belief that teaching was "to create the possibilities for the production or construction of knowledge" (Freire, 1998, p. 30). This philosophy did not negate or undermine Joe's determination to synthesize the feeding and guide students during this process. Joe reminded Pearl of her initial resistance to haiku while acknowledging her public success with the form.

KARINA'S BLUES

Karina was a "fourth-generation New Yorker" of Puerto Rican heritage who referred to the Power Writers as her extended family. Karina's small frame carried within it a large maternal spirit, and she was very protective of her classmates and teachers. She often brought guets of honor to Saturday classes, such as her friends' children, whom she voluntarily babysat. Karina could roll her eyes with the best of them yet flash the brightest smile. She said what was on her mind and considered herself one of the "rocks" of the group. Karina joined the Power Writers at the urging of her friend and fellow Power Writer, Pearl, and the UHHS principal, Dr. Bravo. Pearl, whom Karina called "the oracle" of the Power Writing community, helped Karina edit a letter to the school. Dr. Bravo, or "Brenda," as the students called her, saw a writer in Karina when she received the letter from Karina asking for improved bathroom conditions and more books. "One thing you would expect schools to have is books, and there were none," Karina recounted passionately.

Monday classes gave Power Writers like Karina an opportunity to practice reading and feeding in a smaller group. Sometimes Power Writers would use the smaller venue to practice reading a piece they planned to present to the larger group on Friday. On this day, Karina read a poem about one of her friends who inspired her writing. She explained, "I was just thinking about an old friend of mine that I've known since I was six. He passed away."

> He was my best friend
> My meaning to life itself
> Now there's just a memory of him left
> And the legacy of his so-called wealth
>
> But luxury and cash wasn't the only wealth he had
> Not knowing the innocence he lost would make even the cold-hearted sad
> So to become so rich with love and power
> Soon everyone would envy
> He would soon become a victim of a bad deal gone deadly
> I loved this young man, although a boy
> He grew up way too fast
> Being a child not raised by parents
> People stare as if they don't understand
>
> He was left to fend for self after his parents were killed
> Unknowing of the help that would come
> He was forced to grow up against his will
> Being left with no choice but to do wrong
>
> In order to survive, he must have had an angel
> Who brought him into my life
> We sacrificed for each other
> Like food in his mouth and a pillow for his head
>
> But many nights I went to sleep hungry but satisfied with an overwhelming
>   joy
> As I heard his heartbeat from under my bed
> I gave him my all
> He felt bad that he couldn't give back as much
> But all the money in the world couldn't buy back
> How badly I need to feel his touch

I was his teacher and he was mine
We'll love each other forever
And with a single tear I'll shed
I'll know and he'll know as well
That there will never be another
So with the wonderful memory of you
As I look and gaze into the sky
This is to show my love and appreciation for you
Rest in peace my love, Maliki

After Karina shared her piece, a few of her peers cheered with delight. Since it was a smaller Monday class and many poets were beginning to acclimate to the Power Writing culture, Joe began the feeding process. He addressed Karina's poem but also made eye contact with everyone, as if the feedback was meant for them as well:

If your job was to share with us your sense of loss, you were successful. We want to feed her around the words and the structures. And we want to invite you back to the house so you can get that reading smooth and more singer-like because you definitely are writing songs. Sometimes startlingly beautiful songs. We do this thing where we read at home—so all you have present is you and the words on the page. It's a very beautiful song and it's a Blues. It's clearly a Blues. It's a very beautiful and modern Blues. It's serious and introspective, and it's also about love. A really nice piece of work.

Joe began with a compliment for Karina's articulation of her "sense of loss." He then noted for her peers that they should be thinking about ways to feed her around the "words and the structures." As Joe discussed Karina's poem, he used collective pronouns ("*we* want to invite you back" and "*we* do this thing where *we* read at home") while inviting her back to the "house." In the Power Writing "house," there was a shared value system and commitment that could be carried with you wherever class was held. The "house" served as a metaphor for safety and stability. When Joe invited Karina back to the house, he acknowledged the seminar as a second home for the Power Writers. While feeding Karina, Joe integrated his expectations that the Power Writers would continue to practice outside of class as well as with the larger group. As Joe brought the elements of the Power Writing "house" and instructions for practice together, he also incorporated the imagery of "writing songs," referring to Karina's work as "a very beautiful and modern Blues." Although I discuss the relationship between blues traditions and student poetry more extensively in Chapter 6, it is important to acknowledge the emphasis on reflection.

After feeding Karina, Joe helped her begin the process of feeding her own work:

> JOE: When did he die?
> KARINA: Six months ago.
> JOE: And when were you able to write about that death?
> KARINA: I wrote the piece last week.
> JOE: It took about 6 months for you to write this. Can you think of anything that would have prompted you after 6 months that it became the time? How did you know it was time?
> KARINA: I got my inspiration to write from Maliki because he was always writing. So it's like when he was alive he already knew how I felt about him. I felt that because of his writing that's what got me into writing so the only way I could give back to him and thank him for giving me this form of letting go—this was the only way. By doing this it gave me the strength to let that big gulp go because, to be honest, I was going to stop writing but it's like he gave this to me, so why throw it away? It's the only way I can thank him for giving me such a gift.

Read and feed was not solely about giving and receiving feedback. Power Writers also used the tradition as a way to analyze their own process, as Karina did in this session. Karina talked through her sense of loss or, as she explained, she let go of "that big gulp." Karina and I talked about what it meant to be compared to a "cosmic blues singer":

> MAISHA: I remember when you shared your piece about Maliki, and Joe said you are like a "cosmic blues singer," and it's so true and that piece really, really touches me still. And I want to know what you think about this whole idea when Joe compares your work to a blues singer.
> KARINA: For Joe to give me any compliment, I think, is one of the most wonderful things because Joe has so much knowledge to share; it's kind of overwhelming for one to take in all at one time . . . so for Joe to compliment my writing after so many times of being criticized with "change this" and "change that." It's such a relief—I met my goal. . . . My writing improved after that, and I kept getting compliments because of my good writing. It was because I didn't just write to write. I wrote with emotion, and my emotion and my details in my poetry were set. It was seen, and you could feel it in my writing. And the whole blues and being compared to the blues singers and just being able to sing my life, it's really a compliment to me.
> MAISHA: What does it mean "to be able to sing my life" or being like a blues singer and singing your work? What's the difference between that and just speaking it?

KARINA: When you just speak your poetry, it's not felt by the audience. And that's basically who you try to catch—your audience. And when you sing your poetry, it's when you're singing your life. It's like when you listen to an amateur singer, it's "oh, da-da-da-the end" but when you listen to Mary J. Blige or Mariah Carey or even Alicia Keys, you feel their music through the radio—it's like, oh man, I felt that before and I think that, and it's like you feel it and it's like you're there. It's a feeling you can't explain. You know that it's good and you feel that it's good. And it's there.

Comparing "singing" to the styles found in the music of Mary J. Blige, Mariah Carey, and Alicia Keys, Karina emphasized the importance of being "felt" by the audience as well as trying to "catch" the audience. Karina also contrasted "amateur" singing that did not convey emotion ("oh, da-da-da-the end") with seasoned singing that one could "feel through the radio." Karina's understanding of singing embodies the idea of "performing writing" (Fishman, Lunsford, McGregor, & Otuteye, 2005). Fishman and colleague's characterization of written and performed texts echoes Karina's distinction between "singing" her poetry and "reading it." "When you work with self-performed texts, you work with texts in which lyrics (the what) cannot be separated from the music (the how)" (p. 239). The following vignettes also show Karina as a "feeder" and how she used feedback she had been given to help her fellow Power Writers sing their lives as well.

ELI'S REVOLUTION

Eli joined the Power Writers in the fall semester of 2003 and quickly became a consistent member of the community. Eli earned a reputation among his fellow Power Writers for skipping meals and saving his money to purchase books and music recordings that Joe mentioned in class. Eli told me that he was an "honorary member" of the Puerto Rican community because people never knew how to "categorize" him. Eli humorously recalled telling everyone at a conference for Puerto Rican youth that he was actually El Salvadoran and Colombian and they replied, "You're still one of us." A self-made scholar, Eli actively sought to understand different cultures, religious groups, and music. Joe referred to Eli's journal as a "book of seeds" because of the new directions he was constantly taking in his work. Because of his avid reading and interests in expanding his music collection, Eli's poetry was evolving and reflecting new sounds, words, and ideas. At times, Eli was reluctant to share a piece, believing it was unfinished or needed more work. Joe, however, urged him to let the work go out to the group:

You know, man, you put a lot of pressure on yourself to be perfect and the songs themselves, the stories themselves . . . [have their] own perfection. I think artistic style changes across time. I think the way you find inspiration now and the way you find inspiration 20 years from now will be different. Now, you have certain instincts, and you have a very analytical approach to your work, so spit out the machine. Every day work on it—I think you expect structures to jump out at you and I think more about Lego blocks and then you put the ideas together to build the storybook to sing the song. What do you have today?

Feeding Eli before he actually read his work for the day, Joe urged Eli to "build the storybook" like Lego blocks. Joe wanted Eli to understand that the "songs" and "stories" in his poetry had "their own perfection." Framing writing as an evolution, Joe attempted to give Eli space to be more forgiving of himself if a piece of writing did not come together immediately. As an experienced writer, Joe understood that Eli's writing style would change as he continued to shape and reshape his writing identity. Ultimately it would be the daily practice, according to Joe, that would allow Power Writers to expand their repertoire. Eli responded:

Well, first I'm going to say a quote. I'm going to say a famous quote and then you will hear my poem. "The government has failed us; you can't deny that. Anytime you live in the twentieth century, 1964, and you walkin' around here singing 'We Shall Overcome,' the government has failed us. This is part of what's wrong with you—you do too much singing. Today it's time to stop singing and start swinging."[1] That's by Malcolm X.

> I'll need to hit the books
> Otherwise I'll be missing important things out there when I go out there
>   and look
> Now take a good look
> And all I see here in NYC
> Racism is here
> And sexism is here
> Phobia extraordinaire
> Now take a good look baby
> You just got to be aware
>
> Mama tells me to stay sane in an insane world
> Full of pain
> Where your life is not worth one grain of sand or dust

---

1. Eli quoted Malcolm X's speech "The Ballot or the Bullet," delivered April 1964, in Detroit, Michigan.

Just give me a hand.
Honesty, compassion is a must

Trust me
In order for survival
Our survival
We have to depend on one another
Than to trust our lives in this damned society

It's primal
Rage against everything that's natural in the natural world
Saying shit like hypocrisy
And using/confusing vernacular to have you, him, her and me
Not to think what they say is contradictory

Saddam is captured
Devil studies they've mastered
Like they really give a damn what we say
To them, you're just a slave
In the master's page

I need to hit the books
Otherwise I'll be missing important things out there
Out there I go and look
Nobody cares
But all I see here in NYC is
Racism, sexism, phobia extraordinaire
Just take a good look out there baby
You just have to be aware

That's it.

Everyone went wild with applause. When he closed with a humble "that's it," it seemed as if Eli did not understand his own power. Eli not only chronicled the discrimination he witnessed, but he also achieved a lyrical quality in his work. Eli's declaration also served as a chorus, which was used to close out his piece: "Just take a good look out there baby. You just got to be aware."

Aleyva, a new and soft-spoken Power Writer, began the round of feeding:

ALEYVA: That was strong. That's like "wow!"
ELI: I have another verse, but I did not finish it.
JOE: Thank you, Eli.
KARINA: I got something to say.

JOE: Yeah, speak to him.

KARINA: I thought that your piece was interesting to the point where you actually put your thoughts on the government. When we speak upon the government, it's always you can't say certain things because certain people get offended. To me you didn't care about what we thought about your piece. It was just what you felt and what you think about the topic and if you don't like it, "to hell with you." And I felt that the way you came out was unique because when you talk about what you see and the way you perceived things, the way you look at things, you always have to in one way or another sugarcoat it to make for everybody to see, but you didn't and that's what I liked about your piece. It was real cool.

Karina's feed included her admiration of Eli's willingness to "speak upon the government." Karina also considered Eli's poem to be original and not an attempt to "sugarcoat" his ideas. Eli was one of the first Power Writers to begin the process of linking his personal experiences to national and global issues. He wrote like an ethnographer taking note of everything he saw on the train and in the streets, and transporting his listeners to his world. The musicality in Eli's poem shaped the feeding:

JOE: There's a musical undertone.

ALEYVA: Yeah, it's like there's a beat.

JOE: Always, always.

ALEYVA: It was real nice. It's hard to say—it just shocked me.

MAISHA: There's a lot of music in your style.

KARINA: Yeah!

MAISHA: You're able to achieve that in your work.

JOE: Yeah.

MADDIE: That's why I asked him does he like jazz and stuff.

ELI: I was listening to my mother when I started thinking about this, and when I started writing this, I was listening to Gil Scott Heron.

KARINA: Who?

ELI: Gil Scott Heron. He did "The Revolution Will Not Be Televised." Nobody did a remake of that, but you gotta hear it.

JOE: It's very jazzy.

ELI: Search it in the Internet because the first thing you need to hear is The Last Poets' "When the Revolution Comes" and Gil Scott Heron's "The Revolution Will Not Be Televised."

Like Aleyva, Maddie was new to Power Writers and selective about speaking; however, Eli's poem invoked a response from Maddie. She was keenly interested in Eli's musical inspiration. Eli seized the opportunity to share his recent discovery of The Last Poets and Gil Scott Heron with his classmates. Born after the assassination of Malcolm X, The Last Poets are often hailed as the forefathers of rap. The Last Poets reignited a style that commanded attention, or as Baraka (1996) explained, "This form came out of the revolutionary sixties' Black Arts movement, from way back beyond sorrow songs and chattel wails. Where we created the word as living music. . . . Now the words become a score" (p. xiii). Not only was Eli moving into a political sphere with his poetry, but he was also educating himself about the roots of such work. He was learning that his poetry could be written as music if he desired and could defy categories. For example, Heron has been referred to as both a poet and a jazz or folk musician. Here, read and feed became a forum to exchange new discoveries. I remember being very impressed with Eli's knowledge. My parents, who were community activists in the 1960s and the 1970s, introduced me to these artists, but I do not know if I would have had the discipline and savvy that Eli had to study them on my own. Eli's lesson sparked a discussion about music that absorbed our attention until the end of class. Joe went into a cabinet and pulled out a beautiful picture book about Malcolm X and loaned it to Eli. "When do you want it back?" Eli asked. Shrugging his shoulders, Joe replied, "You know. Whenever you are finished."

KENYA'S DANCE

Whenever I present my work on the Power Writers at conferences such as the National Council of Teachers of English to literacy researchers, teacher educators, classroom teachers, and preservice teachers, someone always expresses concern that students would not respond positively to each other if given opportunities to give each other feedback. For some educators, the idea of not being able to protect a student who has made him- or herself vulnerable is overwhelming. For other educators, the problem may come from their need to have more control over classroom discussions. As a teacher, I understand the temptation to control class discussions; however, I believe it is important to give young people opportunities to share the responsibilities of active listening and providing feedback. How do we teach our students to talk to and teach one another and engage in critical discussions around writing without providing multiple opportunities to practice and become successful? I believe that Black and Brown students are over-policed and micromanaged in urban public schools. Yet as a former teacher of students in magnet and Gifted and Talented Education programs as well as urban classrooms, I know that students in these former classrooms are consistently given opportunities to voice their ideas and have classes built around dialogue and discussion. It is this sense of entitlement that the teachers in the

Power Writing seminar wanted to give students, even if it meant taking risks. Read and feed was not always smooth, but the process was always valuable. This vignette examines what occurred when students and teachers struggled with read and feed and how teachers responded.

In the spring, some of our students started to develop what Roland called the "pig squeal" when poets read serious pieces about their lives. It was as if some of the material in the poetry was too real and the students did not want to acknowledge how some of the work affected them. During a Friday class, Kenya shared a short poem that described her desire to reunite with her father. Kenya, who joined the Power Writing family that year, was a junior. Known for her baby voice and her ability to increase her volume when necessary, Kenya was considered "grown" by her peers. A "fashionista" who wore a different hairstyle nearly every week (thanks to a older brother who was a hairdresser), Kenya carried herself with a great deal of maturity.

Sitting in on a parent-teacher conference between Kenya, her mother, and Joe (with her mother's permission), I witnessed an African American single mother with an uncompromising desire for her daughter to escape the vicious cycles of poverty, teen pregnancies, and failing school. Looking at me and Joe, Kenya's mother emphasized, "I told her to stay way from these kids who can't do anything for you and to graduate on time." Indeed, graduating "on time" was an important accomplishment for most of the young people I met in New York City public schools. Trying to avoid daily distractions caused students to foster a particular set of navigational skills in their neighborhoods. Kenya worked hard to avoid such pitfalls. When Kenya shared "Dance with Me," a poem about missing her father and her desire to reconnect with him, she took a risk with her peers:

> We missed out on a lot of years
> We haven't spoken in almost 10 years
> I try to ignore the fact that you disappeared
> Walked out on the family
> And never cared
> But I forgave because
> If you are gone today or tomorrow
> You will still be recognized as my father
>
> Today is my special day
> And I am honored that you came
> I ask that you take this moment
> To dance with me
> If this is the last time I see you I can say
> I had my dance
> The most important dance of my life

Sweet 16 Father and Daughter Dance
The first dance of the night

Kenya approached a subject that many of her peers knew from personal experience. Her poem was not only a coming-of-age piece, but also a vision and yearning to make peace with her father. Karina acknowledged these characteristics in her "feed":

> Your poem was different from your other poems that you read, that you've written. This one is more serious. And what you tried to–the point you tried to get across is you're not going to dislike him anymore because of what he did because he came to your "Sweet 16." You got that point across. The vision of you dancing with your father–I think you got that across very well because while you were reading your poem I envisioned you dancing with your father. I thought it was a really good poem.

The entire time that Karina was feeding Kenya, students were pretending that they were crying and emotional because of Kenya's poem. In their attempt to act out emotion, a few students were making wailing sounds Karina's important feed was missed by everyone because of the distractions. Although Kenya shrugged it off, Roland, Amy, and I became annoyed and impatient. Roland, visibly disturbed, addressed the class:

ROLAND: The class has developed this horrific pig squeal. What is that?
ROBBIN: We're like crying.
MAISHA: Is it uncomfortable for us to talk about this poem?
ROLAND: Let's go beyond that.
JOE: I think there are two things happening. There's a lot of shared truth in this space right now. Part of the difference between the new people that we've adopted and the old people who have known this for a while is that the truths become heavy. And what I am looking for in all of you is the ability to carry those truths for each other. I agree with you all (looking at me and Roland) that the [pig] squeal is tired. The squeal is tired . . . because we touched something with that . . . when we are dealing with something that has that weight in it, what I really want from you is the utmost concentration to determine where that weight is coming from. Karina gave you, Kenya, an astonishing feed right now in terms of–I think what you said was you know that was real–a real poem. Whenever we are dealing with fathers and mothers in here, it is sensitive material, and we will handle that like men and women.

Joe shifted the focus from the "pig squeal" to the difficult task of feeling the "weight" of some of the shared truths that surfaced in the poetry. Joe was also able to redirect everyone's attention to Karina's feeding of Kenya's poem, which he considered an "astonishing" breakthrough for the class. Joe brought all of us back to the important work of creating a safe space. Not only did the students learn from Joe's feed, but the adults did as well. Roland and I had both been short, but Joe took time to consider the possible reasons that contributed to the "pig squeal" and the uneasiness in the room. Agreeing that the fabricated emotion was "tired," Joe also reminded the Power Writers of their responsibility to the class by emphasizing the fact that Karina "got it" in her feed to Kenya. Power Writers had to (a) contextualize their own responses and struggle to find out the source of those responses, and (b) carry the "weight" for each other so that difficult issues were not isolating and students would not develop a fear of responding. Family issues were regarded as "sensitive material." Handling this material with maturity, "like men and women," was not optional in this classroom community. Joe did not allow students to shirk their responsibility to be respectful of one another. Even with a nontraditional classroom format, Joe asserted his authority and expectations. I believe his ability to stand back, listen, and observe gave him more credibility when he stepped in as the facilitator to remind students why they were there.

CHAPTER FOUR

"We Speak in All Tongues": The Politics of Bronxonics

Karina proudly stood up to share her new poem with Pearl, Jennifer, Amanda, Arline, and Eli. When she read her title, some of the Power Writers asked each other what she had said. Joe asked everyone, "Hello? Hello? Hello? What's up with all that? Did she eat it?" in reference to the way Karina rushed through the title. Slowly and clearly, Karina read her title, "To Whomever It May Concern," for a second time. The Power Writers started clapping and cheering as Joe yelled out, "Yeah, we heard you that time!" After Karina read her poem, Joe addressed the class: "All of you now are poets and singers. You must pronounce every syllable. The message is lost if you do not pronounce the words clearly." However, he warned them about becoming a "monga," which was one of his made-up words for "someone who has something very brilliant to say but can't get it out."

During the feeding for Karina's poem, Amanda told Karina she "likeded it." Everyone knew that Amanda was going to get her "Bronxonics" lesson for the day as well. Before Joe began to "school" Amanda on hypercorrections, she told the class that she knew how to say "liked" but wanted to say "likeded." Through his laughter, Eli told Amanda, "I do that, too." Joe used this opportunity to talk to the class about hypercorrections. However, he punctuated his mini-lecture with "This is a characteristic of Ebonics, Bronxonics—all of which are of equal value to me, but I want you to use it consciously." Everyone seemed to be able to live with this—Joe did not want students using Bronxonics because they did not have access to "Standard English." Instead, Joe told the Power Writers that he wanted them to be armed with a wealth of ways to communicate effectively, "So you can choose."

Revisiting the controversial Students' Right to Their Own Language (SRTOL) resolution adopted by the Conference on College Composition and Communication (CCCC) in April 1974, Kinloch (2005b) reminds composition and literacy research communities that the important work of affirming the linguistic diversity of students, while also providing access to "Standard English," remains a daunting task. Contextualizing SRTOL in the history of higher education's increasing number of "nontraditional" students in the 1970s, Smitherman (1999) asserted that although many of these students did not have "command" of "Standard American English," they had other "communicative strengths—creative ideas, logical and persuasive reasoning powers, innovative ways of talking about the ordinary and mundane" (p. 385). The Power Writers exhibited these communicative strengths in their Bronxonics, which was often heard in their poetry. *Bronxonics*, a term coined by Joe, not only referred to features in "nonstandard" English but also to the cadence, style, and vocabulary used on some of the Power Writers' blocks in the Bronx, influenced by Spanish mixed with English and African American Vernacular English (AAVE). The purpose of this chapter is to examine how Joe addressed issues related to "Standard English" with the Power Writers. I became keenly interested in how Joe attempted to achieve a balance between preparing students for the world outside the Bronx and preserving "around the way" language so they could navigate their neighborhoods and relationships with peers.

Literacy research has offered insight as to how speakers of AAVE can apply their knowledge of language to writing expository texts (Ball, 1992) as well as to interpreting literature in secondary classrooms (Lee, 1995, 2001). Lee argues that many speakers of AAVE have the interpretive skills needed to understand literature from their family and community linguistic practices. In spite of the influence of Black English in Bronxonics, I found that students did not define *Bronxonics* in terms of ethnicity; instead they saw it as a part of the Bronx and their respective neighborhoods, blocks, and buildings. Speaking Bronxonics was not at all unlike speaking AAVE or what Rickford and Rickford (2000) refer to as "Spoken Soul." In fact, one could argue that some people speak Brooklynonics or Harlemonics and so forth. In Power Writing, Bronxonics was originally flagged by Joe and eventually by the Power Writers themselves. Joe's purpose for flagging Bronxonics was not to embarrass or insult students; instead he focused on helping students become conscious of how, why, and when it was used. As recent research on linguistic profiling explains (Alim, 2005; Baugh, 2003), Joe knew that his students would be judged by their ability or inability to articulate themselves skillfully. Joe did not want students to use Bronxonics because it was the only dialect they could access or because they reserved "Standard English" solely for White people:

> I've been in school situations where [students] say "But-but-but, Joe, some-
> times you sound like a white man" . . . and it makes me laugh because it
> opens the door [for] "What do you mean?" And then as long as you are as-
> suming that there is a certain kind of English that only belongs to a certain
> kind of people then you're already trapped. So for me the English language
> belongs to the children. It's our responsibility to teach them the full breadth
> and scope of the language and to never be ashamed of proficiency. And at
> the same time to redefine that proficiency.

Joe's orientation toward "Standard English" and Bronxonics was not as simple as either/or, nor did he assign a hierarchy; he used opportuni- ties—such as when students told him "sometimes you sound like a White man"—to have an open dialogue about language and its uses. Joe's strategy was to unlock the mysteries of language for students, rather than debating these issues with colleagues behind closed doors. Joe started these conversa- tions with his students so they would grow confident in their ability to code- switch. He worked at making students conscious of the politics of Bronxon- ics and challenged them to be prepared to speak to multiple audiences. Joe's approach is one of the healthiest and most productive methods of confront- ing issues of language use. He included his students in the dialogue about what constituted "standard" English. He listened to students carefully in order to discern strategic deviations from the standard for purposeful word choices. In particular settings, students make deliberate choices about lan- guage. As comedian Steve Harvey posits in the documentary *Do You Speak American?*: "I know the correct word is 'isn't' but saying 'isn't' forces my lips to do something I don't what them to do. The word is *ain't*" (2004). As a self-described member of a generation whose parents taught that language would be "used against you," so "get busy," Joe wanted the Power Writers to resist the limitations of only being able to speak "around the way," or in one's familiar circles. However, his disposition toward Bronxonics was still one of respect. As long as students had access to the "standard" and used Bronxonics purposefully, then it was understood to be a valid method of communication:

> Language is a very lush—how do they call it—gumbo. American English is a gumbo. And if we interpret gumbo as a very exotic and spicy stew with ingredients from the entire possibility it had, then we have to accept that there are many, many Englishes . . . that there is an English that is quote-unquote standard, which allows information to be transmitted, but that does not deny the fact that there is information being transmitted all the time in other Englishes.

Using gumbo as a metaphor for thinking about American English, Joe conjures images of an "exotic" and "spicy" stew with many possibilities. Gumbo, a stew that has its origins in Southern cooking, has ingredients that change depending on the individual cook. Joe conceptualizes American English as having many definitions, just like Gumbo. Power Writers redefined literacy by learning how to talk about language issues and deciding when and where to use Bronxonics and for what purposes. This chapter explores how Joe and his students addressed the "many Englishes" in their circle as well as the expectation for literacy beyond their circle. As I began to observe Joe and the Power Writers explore Bronxonics, I wanted to pay close attention to when and where Joe entered the discussions. I also wanted to understand how Joe used the read and feed process and public reading rehearsals to introduce students to new vocabulary and concepts. Finally, I wanted to examine student perspectives on Bronxonics and its uses through formal interviews and informal conversations.

"WIFEN'"

I could never write about Arline without writing about her best friend, Amanda, and vice versa. These two came as a pair. They reminded me of my best friend and me in high school; we were inseparable and always "had each other's back." Both Arline and Amanda had Joe as a teacher in middle school and were excited to reunite with him at University Heights High School. Arline's and Amanda's parents migrated to New York City from the Dominican Republic, and both girls grew up in the Bronx, with Spanish as their primary language. Arline joined the Power Writers during the 2003–2004 school year as an eleventh grader and talked Amanda into joining. Arline was outspoken and warm; she seemed wise beyond her years. Amanda, on the other hand, was soft-spoken and conducted herself with a quiet and dignified beauty that was admired by her peers. Amanda's younger brother and sister came to some of the Saturday sessions and became part of the extended Power Writing family. When Arline introduced her new poem "Wife Beater," Amanda was sitting next to her, cheering her on. Playing on the nickname for men's white tank shirts (traditionally worn underneath dress shirts but increasingly being used as an outer garment), Arline crafted a poem about an abusive relationship:

He got that cute girl he be wifen'
He loves her so much
He hits her with his fists like lightnin'

He knocks you off your feet when you're tired of everything
Next morning you wake up with a swollen eye
And as you cry he hears your sobs
And makes love to you better than the night before

"But he loves me" you say in his defense
Yet dizzy birds roam around your head like animation style
The other day I took you out to have fun
But you barely cracked a smile

He got that cute girl he be wifen'
He loves her so much
He hits her with his fists like lightnin'

But sweetie, stupidity isn't the best defense
Neither is ignorance
He rapes you after you refuse to make love to him

He does it harder and harder
As your tears stream down the side of your face like holy water
As you pray to God to please make him stop

You pray for your life
To be taken away from this earth
But God refuses to listen

As he finishes, he wipes his sweat
And kisses your unloving mouth,
Whispers in your ear, "Baby you know I love you"

And he still got that cute girl he be wifen'

He loves her so much
He hits her with his fists like lightnin'

He pounds on your body
As if practicing for his next match
But he doesn't realize you are his best catch
"But hey girl it doesn't feel as bad as it looks"
Damn girl I feel so much for you
I hope you find a way because on this day
You don't want my help
But I guess that's what I get for trying to be a caring friend
But even though you rejected me
I'll still be there for you
I love you

Arline's poem exercised Bronxonics in two ways. One way was Arline's use of the invariant habitual *be* throughout the poem in her line, "He got that cute girl he be wifen'." Considered "one of the most celebrated features of spoken soul," Rickford and Rickford (2000) argue that the invariant habitual *be* is evidence that African American Vernacular English has its own grammatical system, although *be* in this context continues to mystify linguists (p. 113). In a study of Black English in her college classroom, Jordan (1988) and her students generated guidelines for Black English that included the habitual *be*: "use *be* or *been* only when you want to describe a chronic, ongoing state of things" (p. 130). Jordan and her students also underscored three characteristics of Black English: "the presence of life, voice, and clarity–that testify to a distinctive Black value system" (p 129). Arline also changes voice throughout the poem; at times the poem reads as if the speaker is talking directly to the woman who is being "wifed" and at other times Arline is a narrator. These characteristics are also at the core of Bronxonics and "testify" to multiple experiences of being young, Black, West Indian, Dominican, and Puerto Rican in the Bronx. When Arline and I further discussed her use of "he be" throughout the poem, she had her own theory about her usage:

> Well, the usage of *he be*, as you might know, means "he is" but this is a term that first began in the streets, and it really means that it's done excessively. Usually [*he be*] refers to someone acting out of character, like "He be bugging out." Or to express how you feel about something, to express that you really like something or something that you dislike [as in] "I be hating that." It is basically a slang for a slang. It's another way for us to play around and change language and invent the "misuse" of words to make a statement you can say. It is yet another way for us to create boundaries, like exclusivity, or a distinction between rival boroughs.

What is particularly powerful about Arline's analysis is its emergence from her life experiences to a personal knowledge of this verb supported by her observations of its usage in her neighborhood. More research needs to be conducted on the intersection of AAVE and non–African American students. For Arline, the invariant habitual *be* not only is used when something is done "excessively," as described in Jordan's guidelines for Black English, but Arline also considers it "a slang for a slang." In this context, the invariant habitual *be* serves as a signal phrase verb for introducing a slang expression such as her examples, "He be buggin'" or "I be hating that." Arline further posits that this "misuse of words" is a part of New York City borough rivalry in which creating codes specific to one's borough establishes a sense of "exclusivity." The students took great pride that young people from Queens, Manhattan, and Brooklyn might not be able to understand everything in Bronxonics.

Bronxonics also had its own words and concepts. The second example of Bronxonics in Arline's poem came in the term *wifen'*. Fellow Power Writers seemed to understand Arline's depiction of "wifen'" or being "wifed"; most of the young women nodded their heads in affirmation. I was familiar with the term *wifey* from popular music; this term referenced women whom men considered "wife material." For me the term also signaled a man's sense of ownership of a woman. Joe was fascinated with Arline's use of *wifen'* as a verb and asked Arline to define *wifen'* on her own terms. She explained:

> *Wifen'* around here to me means you got a guy who has a girl, and they've been together for 7 years and he treats her like his wife. [A wifey] is more than a girlfriend but less than a wife. He doesn't give her the respect you give a wife. They probably have three or four kids. There's not the equal partnership that a husband and wife have. He takes her places but not to the nicest places. I haven't really gone outside the area, but I am talking about here. I know people who have been wifen' their partner for like 10 years. It's just a regular thing. You don't see married couples anymore, and you think that's in the movies but it's not.

Arline clarified that *wifen'* had a specific meaning "around here," or in her neighborhood. Using Bronxonics—in this case, the word *wifen'*—allowed Arline to tell the truth about a type of relationship that she found problematic—a woman who was "more than a girlfriend" and "less than a wife." A "wifey," or a woman who was being "wifed," was expected to raise children and be in a committed and monogamous relationship with an abusive man who took her to places but "not to the nicest places." Arline believed that this arrangement led many of her peers to believe marriage was only "in the movies" or on television. She knew from her own parents, however, that marriage was possible and real. The reality was that students witnessed *wifen'* daily, and there was no word in "Standard English" that could provoke the emotion and understanding that *wifen'* accomplished in the context of Arline's poem. When I asked Arline and Amanda about their views on Bronxonics, they began their own dialogue:

> AMANDA: [Our teachers] look at [Bronxonics] as "what kind of language are you using?" I guess [Joe] wants us to use proper English sometimes.
> ARLINE: When Joe tells us [that's] "Bronxonics" [he's saying] it's our culture and it's a part of us.
> AMANDA: When we get older and we get into our career, [Joe] doesn't want us to use it. He wants us to be proper and show them we're coming from the hood *and* we know how to talk. I guess he wants us to know when to use it and when not to use it.
> ARLINE: I think he does want us to use it. He's saying adapt to your environment. Let people know you are street smart and book smart.

Both Arline and Amanda understood that Joe wanted his students to "know when to use [Bronxonics] and when not to use it," or to learn how to "adapt to your environment." Looking into her future and the possible future lives of her peers, Amanda saw Joe's flagging of Bronxonics as a way to differentiate communication in one's "hood" and in one's "career." Ultimately, Arline and Amanda's characterization of Bronxonics demonstrated multiple ways of knowing and multiple ways of being that did not have to be in conflict. I do not believe this can be emphasized enough. Many young people want to know that "street smarts" and "book smarts" can coexist. Is it possible for classroom communities to cease presenting these two "smarts" as dichotomous? Many students in urban public schools fear choosing one over the other. Joe emphasized to me, Roland, and Amy how important it was to not leave our students "naked" when putting them out into the world; if they were completely stripped of Bronxonics, they would be less adept at navigating their communities and we could not do that for them. Joe taught the Power Writers that they could have both discourses and change them like articles of clothing for specific occasions. Creative words were only one feature of Bronxonics. Another feature of Bronxonics included hypercorrections.

"I LIKEDED IT!"

Catalina, or "Cat," was the "baby" of the Power Writing family. She joined the Power Writers as a ninth grader and was considered the "baby" because of her age and also her sweet voice. Born in the Bronx, Cat was raised by her mother and father, who migrated to New York City from the Dominican Republic. Cat's parents and older sister attended all of the public readings, screaming loudly from the moment Cat's name was called until Cat spoke her first word. Whenever I saw Cat's mother, she always greeted me with an endearing "Hola, Mami" and complimented my Spanish even when my grammar was lacking. Cat had a lot to say about race and being mistaken for a "Black girl." She saw herself as a pioneer in moving beyond skin tone and hair texture. Recruited to Power Writing by Pink (a first-generation Power Writer), Cat recalled, "I was in math class and [Pink] saw me writing and invited me to Power Writing. I had love issues and family issues." Cat was famous for using the classic Bronxonics phrase "I likeded it" when feeding her peers. Power Writers "corrected" each other when something like this happened. During read and feed, Karina "caught" Cat using this feature of Bronxonics:

> CAT: I likeded it.
> KARINA (to Cat): It's *liked*.
> ROBBIN (to Cat): You said *likeded*?
> KARINA: Yes, she said *likeded*. It's *liked*.
> JOE: Wait a minute. Hello. Cat, let me jump on this discussion. Look, for the new people, one of our jobs, one of our goals . . . no matter how we speak around the way the way we speak around the way is magic and money, and it helps to keep us in the world, but there are other places where we have to take this.

When Joe addressed Bronxonics, he used subjective and objective personal pronouns: "the way *we* speak around the way . . . helps to keep *us* in the world." He used both humor and serious tones when discussing language. However, Joe was consistent about the option to choose. In order to choose, a writer had to know and understand his or her choices. Joe portrayed "around the way speak" or Bronxonics as "magic and money." Bronxonics was "magic" because it catches attention and sometimes finds its way off the block, perhaps in a song or a movie, and may eventually be validated by the American public as a word. Bronxonics was "money" because it held currency on the block, and it "redefined proficiency" in that context. This "dialect" had the power for students to get what they wanted and needed in their immediate worlds. At the same time, Joe helped students understand that communication in the larger world functioned outside the musicality of Bronxonics. Again, Joe underscored the importance of having both currencies without assigning a hierarchy. Joe continued to address Cat's use of the term *likeded*:

> So, what young Cat is doing is what a linguist would call a "hypercorrection." She wants to be *sooooo* right that the past tense of the word *like* is *liked* so she says "likeded"—*more* than *like* in the past. So what we try to do is this,

we never look down on you in terms of your language, but what we do with your language is we shape it like we were sharpening knives so that you'll have use of the word *liked* and also *likeded,* but *likeded* has to have a reason and a function that only *likeded* can do. Thank you, Karina, for letting me jump in.

As he contextualized Cat's use of *likeded,* Joe wanted the students to understand Cat's desire to be "more than right." Joe explicitly discussed *hypercorrections* as a technical term used by linguists. By doing this, Joe made working toward proficiency in "Standard English" possible; "we shape [language] like we were sharpening knives." This image invited students to consider language a tool, something that each of them could maintain and develop. Shaping language was part of becoming a "Jedi of words" while defining and redefining proficiency.

When I interviewed Cat and asked her about the read and feed process, she explicitly addressed how it helped her make decisions about language: "Feeding helps put my mind in focus. . . . I try to listen and try to understand. So that helps me. . . . They still tease me about 'I likeded it.' It aids to speak better to them and make sure they know I understand what they read to me." What I always find powerful about the exchange among Cat, Robbin, and Karina is how Joe shifted the power and agency back to the students by showing his appreciation for Karina's "letting" him "jump in" the read and feed circle for Cat. Here, Joe signaled to his students that Power Writing really belonged to them. Inviting students to take ownership of the class was not in conflict with his responsibility to "jump in" when and where needed.

"¿Y QUE?"

The currency of Bronxonics also lived within students' bilingualism. In fact, Joe wanted students to think of their neighborhoods and linguistic diversity as the "Bronx Diaspora." He would discuss at great length themes from everyone's culture, including music and religious practices. Joe's premise was that "we speak in all tongues," as he explained to the Power Writers at the beginning of the semester: "I don't want you to worry about grammar at this point, although later we will become crazy about it." Setting the pace for the class, Joe foreshadowed his expectations for grammar. However, before he got "crazy" about grammar, Joe wanted to assign topics in which the students could be experts. One of the assignments aimed at describing this Bronx Diaspora was to write a poem about race, answering the question "How do I feel about race in my neighborhood, city, country and the world?" Joe's assignment invited students to understand how diverse the group was in languages and experiences:

Look at you. The gene pool in this room has every kind of human possible. Okay? Does everybody understand that? What a wonderful room this is. The DNA in this room speaks for this species. Not a simple issue. For those of you who write in more than one language . . . you need to say what you need to say. You need to say what you need to say.

Many of the Power Writers were fluent in both English and Spanish and were encouraged to translate their pieces or to use words from their mother tongue. I was surprised to learn that students referred to any Spanish-speaking person as "Spanish," in order to generalize across different Latino or Hispanic groups. Most of the bilingual Power Writers wrote their poetry in English, while some of their peers used Spanish words to preserve particular meanings they believed could not be translated. I learned from Spanish-speaking Power Writers that they considered their bilingualism part of their identity. Not one student could recount any issues in learning English and Spanish. Torres-Guzmán examined the way Puerto Rican students move between English and Spanish, asserting, "Bilingualism is a manifestation and expression of self-determination within in the context of the United States" (Torres-Guzmán, 2004, p. 120). Similarly, many of the Dominican students in Power Writing considered bilingualism to be part of their identity because they would face marginalization if they were not fluent in Spanish. Arline of ten inserted Spanish phrases into her work, as did her classmate Kari. Raised in the Bronx by Dominican parents, Kari frequently came to class adorned in a rhinestone-studded belt with her name on it and a "name plate" on her gold chain that read "Kari" in ornate cursive writing. Kari boldly raised questions about people's preoccupation with ethnic categories. She was proud of her Dominican heritage and challenged her peers to be cautious about making assumptions based on race. Because she had a fair complexion, Kari considered herself a target for such assumptions. In her poem "Race," Kari confronted racism by asking "*¿Y que?*" or "And what?" in her community. Kari selected this piece to read at the first public reading of the 2003–2004 school year:

Looking around
And seeing how others are treated
Just because I'm this color
Does it bother you? Does it matter?
Why is it a problem if I'm Dominican, Black or Chinese?
Does it matter if I'm Spanish?
People suffering because of their skin color
Being Black, is it a problem? I think not.
If you find him, her or them so different, why?
Why do white have to be "right" and Black "in the back"?
Does that sound right to you? I think not.

Why are we racist? Being racist is part of the world.
But should it be here? Hmph. Ask me and it better be, "I think not"
People who are racist don't see that they are dehumanizing themselves
Don't they know this?
It don't matter if I get married to a Black person
I was raised by Dominicans, I hear the racism all the time
Why you must be that way? That's a question you, me all of us ask
Nobody knows the answer.
I know I'm tan and for that some might think I'm white
But guess what? I might be Black.
But do you care? Hell no. You're too busy looking at my complexion.
And assuming I'm Hispanic
Assuming, Hmph you get it? Making an ass out of yourself
But yeah, I'm Hispanic
¿Y que? And what?
I could be Black and proud
¿Y que? And what?
Tell me something now

This was a breakout poem for Kari, who accepted Joe's challenge to confront racism as well as "classically negative" statements that people made
about Blacks. Kari took advantage of Joe's encouragement that "you need to
say what you need to say" whether it was in English, Spanish, or Bronxonics.
For example, in a memorial poem for her grandfather, Kari addressed him
as "*mi papa*" throughout the poem, starting a new tradition of infusing her
primarily English poetry with Spanish words, phrases, and terms of endear-
ment. In "*¿Y que?*" Kari courageously named the racism found in her own
family, peers, and her neighborhood. "*¿Y que?*" was more than a question in
Kari's poem; it was a declaration of antiracist principles and a challenge to
those who were "too busy" looking at her complexion or who discriminated
against their own.

Language use in the classroom will remain a controversial topic for teachers and teacher educators; this issue incites some of the most passionate discussions in my curriculum and instruction seminar for preservice teachers every year. Some would argue that Bronxonics, African American Vernacular
English, and other language practices deemed "non-standard" do not have
a place in the English language arts classroom. In Power Writing, Bronxonics was an effective tool to discuss linguistic diversity among students. Joe
demonstrated how much he valued his students' language practices while
simultaneously requiring students to learn how to articulate why they chose
particular words in particular contexts. As long as Power Writers were making strategic choices and building their repertoire, Joe was satisfied. Power

Writers were learning how to be sophisticated code-switchers who could take pride in their ability to adapt and adjust to any situation while preserving the integrity of the words, styles, and cadence they felt most comfortable using. In the next chapter, I examine how Joe helped students develop new vocabulary to add to their repertoire using his "catching" or "fishing for" words method.

CHAPTER FIVE

Joe's Griots and "Exotic Dah-Dah": Learning How to "Catch" Words

After hearing so much about the Power Writers and their poetry, my younger brother Damany decided to make a special trip to New York City and attend class. Everyone was excited about meeting "Maisha's brother," and I told Damany ahead of time that all "guests" had to participate in the read and feed process. I do not think he really understood what this meant until he was asked to feed Yari for her uncharacteristically short poem, which included some choice words. After a long pause, Damany fed Yari, saying, "I think there's something to be said for brevity." Joe immediately jumped in and exclaimed "bre-WHAT?" Damany repeated himself as Roland quoted Shakespeare's famous line

in Hamlet, *"Brevity is the soul of wit." Yari asked if "brevity" had something to do with "brave," which prompted Amy to get up and write* brevity *on the board. All eyes were on Damany, and the Power Writers erupted into laughter because they knew it was time to "catch words," and* brevity *was definitely a new word. Joe gave his famous line, "I'm sorry, but my gold tooth is hurting," which signaled that he needed a definition for* brevity. *He further explained to an unsuspecting Damany, "A while back, my students were wearing gold fronts in their mouths but would sit back in class and not contribute." Referring to the temporary teeth jewelry that students wore as part of a fashion trend, Joe gave students a hard time about having what appeared to be expensive dental work without having something worth saying that could potentially "show it off." Acknowledging Damany's contribution to building the Power Writers' vocabulary, Joe explained to everyone that learning new vocabulary was a form of decolonization: "It's about being free—free from what the culture is trying to ascribe to us."*

In a study of how race, language, and culture intersected in his Philadelphia high school English classroom, Fecho (2004) described his skepticism about the role of vocabulary in a small learning community. Fecho explained that many students were able to memorize lists and score well on quizzes, but he saw little correlation between high quiz scores and confidence in language use. Given the "weight of tradition and conventional wisdom about SATs," Fecho also believed that he could not completely omit vocabulary from his teaching (p. 17). Like Fecho, Joe, Roland, Amy, and I grappled with how to introduce vocabulary in meaningful and productive ways.

One of the salient characteristics of Power Writing was the act of "fishing for," or "catching," words. Power Writers were expected to inquire about every word they did not recognize or understand. It was not clear if students actually understood Joe's additional mission to "decolonize" their thinking; however, the Power Writers did understand that part of their responsibility was to fill up their journals with new words and meanings and eventually to implement them into their own writing and speaking. Joe had signature methods that he used to signal that it was time to fish for words. The first method was using his hands to mimic holding a fishing rod; Joe would dramatize reeling in a fish (or, in this case, a word). Depending on the word, he might convey more of a struggle if it was "exotic" and less if he suspected that students had some background knowledge. Another method Joe used was to engage co-teachers and visitors in defining words and concepts. Joe sometimes staged dialogue around vocabulary with adults in the room (much like the opening narrative in which my unsuspecting brother was featured). Joe's process of using other adults in the room as props as he staged discussions around words helped the Power Writers see how people made sense of unfamiliar vocabulary.

This chapter demonstrates how the Power Writers cocreated a tradition of collecting words with the guidance of teachers and mentors. My questions about the practice of "fishing for" or "catching" words emerged from the data: How was spoken word poetry used to introduce new vocabulary words and concepts? How did the teaching team use student writing to access new words and ideas? First, I show how Joe used an original composition to challenge students to catch words. Next, I offer an example of catching literary devices with a teaching team. Finally, I show how the students challenged themselves and took ownership of the catching-words process as a result of a field trip.

THE UPRISING

In a chapter titled "The Weekly Test," Dahl (1947) depicts a puritanical headmaster, Ms. Trunchbull, and an enthusiastic new teacher, Miss Honey, in his well-known children's book *Matilda*. Ms. Trunchbull quizzes students on spelling while pulling their ears and berating them in front of their classmates. When Ms. Trunchbull learns of Miss Honey's attempts to use poetry in spelling and vocabulary instruction, she chastises the new teacher, "And anyway you're not meant to teach poetry when you're teaching spelling. Cut it out in the future, Miss Honey." Miss Honey bravely responds, "But it does teach them some of the harder words wonderfully well" (p. 147). Joe's approach to vocabulary and spelling was unconventional. Like Miss Honey, Joe saw potential in using a medium that students enjoyed.

A week after the Power Writers' first public reading of the 2003–2004 school year, Joe shared his poem "Tuesday Night Uprising." This poem was a tribute to the Power Writers' commitment to their writing and performance on a snowy Tuesday night at Roland's loft. Joe's poem was more than a praise song; it was a map of a new world with complicated references and intertextuality. In addition to praising the Power Writers, Joe's poem also introduced new words, concepts, and history. Joe never dumbed down his writing, and I probably had as many questions about Joe's references as the students did. "Tuesday Night Uprising," like "Nuyorican Poets Café, East 3rd Street, Atlantis" (see Chapter 1), placed the Power Writers at the center. Joe gave the Power Writers some guidelines:

> I want you to look for unfamiliar words. Some of the words are names of mythical figures. Okay? So if you don't know—this is like an insider joke for writers. At the same time, from the bottom of my heart, I wrote this poem for you all. So, therefore, if this was the kid's version I would footnote it, but I don't want to treat you like kids, so I want you to listen to the poem, please.

Presenting his poem as an "insider joke for writers" invited Power Writers to view themselves as part of a writing community. Joe was letting his students in on the "joke," introducing them to the ways writers use references to convey multiple meanings in their work. He also named the duality in his purpose for the poem: Indeed, the poem was a tribute to the students' "uprising," but it was also an opportunity to catch words. Joe foreshadowed the students' need to listen attentively in anticipation of lines that he would normally footnote. He wanted to read through the poem without stopping so students would be able to hear it in its entirety. There was no time for rest; Joe maximized every resource and used his poetry to celebrate and illustrate.

In many of our discussions and debates on our train rides from the Bronx to Harlem, Joe and I talked about the sense of urgency we felt as secondary educators to get students in urban public schools "caught up." I compared and contrasted my experiences as a first-grade teacher and tenth-grade English teacher. When I taught first grade, I was excited by the potential I saw in the children in my classes. As a secondary teacher, I continued to see possibilities for my students, but I was overwhelmed by how little time I had to get my young people prepared for life beyond the classroom walls. In a compelling story of "hoop dreams" and inner-city nightmares, Frey (1994) inspires yet haunts readers with the image of one young man who never parts with his SAT vocabulary flashcards. I found myself inspired by the young man's dedication and commitment to learning the words. At the same time, this image disturbs me because as the narrative unfolds, Frey forces readers to realize that this young man is in a race against time, frantically trying to make up for years of substandard schooling. Joe shared similar sentiments. He felt that by the time students got to Power Writing, he had to "undo" years of miseducation and the lack of self-confidence that resulted from not being given a chance to imagine possible lives. Vocabulary and the ability to use it, according to Joe, functioned as critical building blocks for developing confidence. Joe read through "Tuesday Night Uprising" twice:

> The sun dives through antique windows into the west
> and its fading light reveals the eyes of young poets
> which are filled with the light of true story
> They are calling the people to this celebration of life
> an act older than writing
> and Bibles
> and Korans
> and Torahs
> and certainly older than money

Their eyes dancing in story's blue light
It's fire pushing back the night
Anansi and bubalah take seats in corners
Coyote wails
Ancient griots with their hands enmeshed in mnemonic strings
glide in and
Out of shadow
Thoth's baboon grin flashes
Unseen, yet witnessing silently
The songs of the young calling and calling and calling in the voice of gated
Windows and nightmare and hopes and dreams and dissatisfactions
On the podium an invincible Tower of Babel
The real United Nations of a just world called to order
Poems like hymns
Like Psalms
Like the night lotus unfolding
Like sermons
The poems take flight in the night air and erupt and re-erupt
From faces unlined by time and minds unscarred by the cynicism of our
Metallic and
    Mercantile now
Word after word line after line in tone after tone
The new ghost dance is mastered
It calls for a new world
That can never be
Unless we dream it
Sing it
Live it
and
Poem it
into being
A world of the free
the home of the brave
Literate and enchanted
All clothed in the beauty of loves wisdom
Forever
And ever
Be poetry[1]

In Joe's poem, his students were strategically placed within a continuum of literate traditions that was "older than money." In Joe's tribute to students, the word *poem* was a verb signaling his students' ability to write the new world

---

1. This is not Joe's final version of "Tuesday Night Uprising," but it is the transcribed version from this particular class session.

they imagined, or "poem it into being." This "literate and enchanted" world, according to Joe, was their right as students in American public schools.

Joe believed in these young people beyond imagination; he did what I always believed strong teachers do—he saw the potential in young people sometimes before they were able to see it in themselves. Elsewhere I write about the intergenerational and crossgenerational traditions in open mic communities; elder poets helped younger poets view themselves as the next generation of writers and as historians of their culture through writing (Fisher, 2003b, 2004, 2006). I argue that these relationships helped newer poets develop their identities as writers because their work was valued, respected, and on some level cherished by their mentors. Recognizing in the students some reluctance to begin the read and feed process, Joe staged a vocabulary dialogue with me, beginning with the Anansi reference:

KARINA: Hmph.

JOE: That's really what I have to say to you all. And Maisha, because she's the one with the training, knows who all those figures are. So Anansi, what comes to your mind?

MAISHA: Anansi—the folkloric tales—the spider. The Anansi Tales. People call them "Nansi Tales" too because they either could not pronounce *Anansi* or it sort of got lost in the translation.

JOE: Actually, in English Creole, they just dropped the vowel. Can anyone spell it? Spell what you hear. The figure is called *Anansi*.

ARLINE: A-n-a-n-s-e-y?

JOE: Very close. The phonemics are right.

JASMINE: A-n-a-s-e-y?

JOE: You did the same thing she did. The "s" sound is a hard sound.

KARINA: I don't know.

JOE: Come on. You know it.

KARINA: A-n- . . .

PEARL: A-n-a-n-s-i.

JOE: Anansi is the teacher of truths. The next word, *bubalah,* is Yiddish. What is Yiddish?

KARINA: Isn't it Jewish?

JOE: A Jewish what?

ARLINE: Not a language?

JOE: Yes, it's an Eastern European language. Jewish people spoke Yiddish. Can someone spell it, or should we look it up?

PEARL: Y-i-d-d-i-s-h.

JOE: Get that on film, Maisha! The National Spelling Bee!!!

JOE (to Karina): How do I spell it?

KARINA: Y-i-d-d-i-s-h

MAISHA: You guys are really good spellers. You'd be surprised how many people make it through without being good spellers.

JOE: About Karina. Karina *be* fast. You know what I'm saying? Sometimes in class *they're* not fast enough for *you*. . . . Because American English has so many influences, it's your job to learn them all.

The Power Writers could have spent the entire semester working on Joe's poem. Joe did the initial fishing with "Anansi the Spider" by purposefully putting me ("with all the training") on the spot. Joe hoped to validate Anansi's legacy by soliciting my knowledge about this legendary folk character. The initial fishing was also an invitation to become involved in the process. Asking students to work on spelling provided opportunities to experience some success before moving to the difficult task of explicating the poem. Spelling was still an art in Power Writing, and students were encouraged to work at it. Returning to the job description for becoming a Jedi of words, Joe reminded students that American English has multiple influences, alluding to the discussion of Yiddish words. Explicating poetry is no easy task, regardless of age, grade, or experiences; however, the Power Writers were invested in all of the words and concepts in "Tuesday Night Uprising," because Joe wrote it for and about their poetry and performance. They had a purpose for "getting it." During Monday class and again in a larger Friday class, Power Writers wrestled with the concepts in the poem. Referring to the new concepts as "exotic dah-dah," Joe's purpose was not to undermine the importance of unfamiliar words but to encourage students to be fearless when approaching new vocabulary.

JOE: Okay. Any exotic dah-dah? What's the next word that got by everybody?
PEARL, KARINA, and JENNIFER: *Mnemonic.*
JOE (smiling): Okay. That's a good one. That's a good one.
JENNIFER: How do you spell [*mnemonic*]?
JOE: That's one that you have to be a speller to spell. . . . I don't want to spell that one yet because that's the $20,000 question. And in your spelling of *mnemonic*, if you've never seen it before you will be shocked. But you all know what mnemonic devices are. All of you. All of you know. I don't know if some of you know that some African storytellers have something that looks like a cat's cradle. Everybody know what a cat's cradle is? (Joe held his hands up and interlocked his fingers creating an illusion of tapestry.)
KARINA: No.
JOE (Holding his hands up and mimicking the practice of the cat's cradle game): You know when you play the string game?
A FEW STUDENTS: Oh yeah!
PEARL: I like that.
JOE: Except their strings are attached someplace on the wall and they have

objects, and the function of the objects is to help the storyteller
remember the story. . . . Mnemonic devices are what you use to help
you memorize.

Like many literary devices and terminology, Joe underscored his belief
that students knew what a mnemonic device was, even if they had not heard
of the term. Similar to Lee's (1995, 2001) work with cultural modeling in
urban high school English classrooms, Joe's method embraced the idea that
students unlocked the mysteries of language daily through their music and
their exchanges with peers and family. Joe wanted to help his students develop a vocabulary to name these practices and methods to gain confidence in
using such tools. Joe also distinguished between words that could be spelled
phonemically and words that "you have to be a speller to spell." Students did
not have to be ashamed of not knowing how to spell *mnemonic,* and Joe was
pleased that the students chose this word and assured them that it was not a
conventional spelling. Joe also used his own dramatization and mnemonic
device to explain the function of the term.

JENNIFER: I had another one. [*Griot*]?
JOE: Oh! *Griot?*
JENNIFER: Yes.
MAISHA: Yeah. I thought that came before *mnemonic.* I had it, too.
JOE (teasingly): I thought it was a combination of grits and oats together. Per-
    haps I'm mistaken. No one knows what a griot is?
JENNIFER: No.
JOE: You listen to those hard rappers. I've heard them use the word *griot.* . . .
    A griot was a person who, when cultures kept their records orally, if you
    were trained to be a griot you learned the epic poem that was a history
    of your people. . . . A griot was the "rememberer" of people's stories.
ARLINE: So it would be their job to pass it down?
JOE: Yes. Ultimately they would pass it down. Like if your grandmother was
    telling a story, and she couldn't remember how her mother ended it she
    would go to the griot. The griot would go, "We tell this story for different
    seasons and different reasons and it has multiple endings. This is the sto-
    ry. These are the multiple endings." Okay? That person had a fantastic
    capacity for memory. So today there are people in cultures where they
    may memorize the Koran.
KARINA: The Koran is what? A bible for what?
JOE: For the Muslims.
JENNIFER: Yes. My dad's family studies the Koran.

Tempted to begin a discussion about the history of religion, Joe stopped
himself, saying, "I'm not going to go there right now," because he wanted to

stay focused on vocabulary. This was a reminder for me about why so many teachers concentrate their vocabulary efforts in an orderly way. Sitting with students and tackling words line by line takes time, patience, and an enormous amount of commitment. Explicating poetry line by line could also take the group in a different direction with every line. In order to define *griot*, Joe offered his own word, *rememberer*. This play on the word *remember* worked for Arline and provided her with the context clue she needed to understand the role of a griot. When Arline perked up and started to define a griot's job, she created an opportunity for Joe to elaborate. This process was infectious, and I joined the discussion (which was part of Joe's plot all along):

> MAISHA: I recently read some things about griots that I thought were really interesting. They also were praise singers, and they would act as sort of the messenger between the community people and whoever the leader was. So, say, for example, the leaders were not doing what they're supposed to do, the griot [would] create a song that praised the leader and complimented them. It's not that the leader has really earned it, but it's to say, "We actually want you to do these things." They almost make the leader feel guilty in a way.
>
> JOE (smiling): "These are the characteristics of a real leader."
>
> MAISHA: Right. Right. Like "Oh leader, this that and the other. You do this for us. You do that."
>
> ARLINE: And he realizes he's not doing it so he's like, "Oh let me do that."
>
> MAISHA: Exactly.
>
> JOE: Excellent. Excellent.
>
> MAISHA: So that's a really important part of the griot. And also something that I think is really interesting with respect to griots is that they were also sometimes outcasts in their communities.
>
> JOE: Yes.
>
> MAISHA: And so as much information and history and missing links they preserved, in many cases they were marginalized.
>
> JOE: Particularly in modern times.
>
> MAISHA: Yeah.
>
> JOE: Particularly in modern times, okay? Because the story—the true story of the world's peoples—is aborted in the age of colonialism. And so some of the authors I want you guys to read deal with the issues of what happens to people, what they become—politically and socially dominated people. And all of the traditions lose their mores at times. Any more exotic dah-dah?

At this point, defining *griot* evolved into a conversation about the history and role of the griot in West African culture. I fell into Joe's vocabulary trap. He wanted students to see what process looked like, which I believe builds a compelling case for team teaching in English language arts classrooms.

Engaging in a discussion and role-play of how a griot or praise singer might translate the desires of a community to its leader, Arline was able to make an offering to the definition. Joe was always careful to bring the conversation together at some point without getting too far away from the original purpose by reminding students of their role and responsibilities in class.

RON'S STREAM OF CONSCIOUSNESS

An alumnus of UHHS and a student at Bronx Community College, Ron returned to his alma mater to attend Power Writing on Mondays and Fridays. Born and raised in the Bronx and of African American heritage, Ron would seldom laugh and joke with his peers, but he could be seen long after class still engaging Joe in philosophical discussions about global issues or even what was happening on "the block." Ron consistently brought work to Roland and Joe for more feedback. In fact, when I interviewed Ron for this project, he met me at my office at Teachers College with a writing portfolio that contained his original poetry chronologically arranged, which he had been keeping since middle school. Images of drugs—crack cocaine in particular—and guns haunted Ron's poetry, but they were never portrayed in glory. These forces were met by a second voice in his poetry that offered women in white, water, and babies as tools to erase the damage caused by drugs and violence. Students were tormented by Ron's poetry; they respected the work tremendously but did not fully grasp his concepts. He stated, "My poem's called 'Vivian'."[2]

> I smoke the crack
> Tears line my drink
> My thoughts start shaping the drink
> Niggas look at me and say I'm regular
> But I just wanted crack that seems irregular
> Crack crawls in my absent world where the women lay naked, horny
> But abstinent in this ignorance of new pleasure
> The pusher looked me in the eye
> The crack slowly becoming . . .
> As my grandmother watched me she probably seen me in her
> Her heroine-addicted eyes reappear
> The crack made me a prisoner in the white, polluted circumstance
> How they make me love the drug
> How they make me love the pusher
> But train me to hate myself
> But to love gold that don't push us

---

2. "Vivian" is a pseudonym.

I fiend for the pipe just like my grandmother
That pipe told me stories
The pipe kidnapped me
Like I had an affair with it
Marks on my arm
Niggas looking at the blood from my nose
Plus it felt like someone was holding a gun next to me
You lookin' at Vivian's eyes
They burn like matches
They drugged my brain with mental injections
The absence I feel through my black veins
I feel the shit that brushes against my project windows
Yeah black families got crack heads in their families
But that's just how they want to kill us
I don't want to die
I looked at the pusher's eyes
Like they were kilos
Looking at the lonely women
How come they can't hold me
While the pusher get paid
As I kissed Vivian she sells me her drug
Only to kill her grandson
The kiss of my reflection stops my fiendin'
My reality is scaring me
Like I'm dead, like Vivian
I'm on drugs like my grandmother

Power Writers always had trouble feeding Ron. I believe that students stopped listening at some point when they decided they could not understand his poems. Ron's poetry was immersed in the sadness of drug addiction, violence, and the yearning to put lives together shattered by crack cocaine. In Jamal Shabazz's photographic essay *A Time Before Crack* (2005), photos of teenage love, hip hop crews, and young men and women striking poses with beaming smiles provide a window on what New York City was like before communities were infested by crack cocaine. Ron's poetry, on the other hand, was a photographic montage of a time after crack cocaine, when it festered in the minds and bodies of the users and the memories of the witnesses. Sadly, I knew the images in Ron's poetry too well, since I came of age in the 1980s; my block saw its first "crack heads" or "dope fiends" when I started middle school. It was as if entire families disappeared from our block—not just physically but emotionally as well. It was painful beyond words to know that Ron's generation was strangely familiar with these same images:

ALEYVA: I was lost! [Laughter] Like, I don't even know. I was lost. It was good, though. I like the way you said it and how you flow with it, but I was lost.

JENNIFER: I would agree with Alevya. I was trying to look at him to see if I could catch on, but really, I was lost. It was too long, and I was trying to picture how he was thinking, but at the same time I got lost in that.

KARINA: Um, [Ron], I thought your poem, like your other poems, was very, very strong. I felt that the majority of your poems, your writings, works has to do with your everyday life, and I've come to realize there's a lot of drugs around you. Using that in your writing I feel is great only because you get to get that thought out there and let people know what you are going through instead of keeping it all to yourself. I felt that it was excellent. If you keep writing that way, you are going to lose a lot of people because your writing is very powerful but at the same time it's very long. The first couple of images we can get, then after that we kind of lose you. I find you again but . . .

RAMON: I'd like to comment on that.

JOE: We need to add to this.

KARINA: I love it, though.

RAMON: You know, I'll be honest. It takes a while to get Ron, but once you do, it's there. It's not like you're gonna get it the first couple of months. It took me a whole year. It's only this year that anything that comes out of his mouth [and] I understand it. Last year I was completely lost. You just have to find that piece every time he reads and pay attention to what he's saying. Look at the bigger picture—don't look at just the words.

KARINA: I understand that but– [inaudible]

ROLAND: Maybe I could help a little bit. In literature there's a kind of writing that is sometimes called "stream of consciousness." Have you heard of that phrase before?

SOME STUDENTS: Yeah.

POWER WRITER: I just don't know what it means.

JOE (pointing to student journals): Do we need to collect? A stream of consciousness to me sounds like something running in the gutter.

ROLAND: Well, we know what *consciousness* means. When you're awake, you are conscious, and *stream* we know, so it's as if you were to–if someone were to open your mind, right? And at the moment they opened the door to your mind, whatever is in your mind, whatever would start to pour out, you would write [it] down. In a stream. Like a stream just runs. It's a series of words, a series of images. Not necessarily organized the way we've been taught to organize things in school with a beginning, a middle, an end, a theme, etcetera. But it's the way, sort of the flow of ideas and thoughts and images in your mind.

AMY: It's unedited.

ROLAND: It's unedited. It's a way to help you to try to understand—I
    think—the work that Ron is doing. Ron is tapping into his own stream of
    consciousness. What happens sometimes is that when you go into that
    space, all sorts of things happen. You get repetitions of images of lan-
    guage. It isn't necessarily easy to follow. And it doesn't make sense the
    way we're taught to make sense. But, like Ramon says, eventually that
    stream begins to flow over you and you begin to feel it. It's like listening
    to music. You're not getting a specific set of clear ideas in the music but
    you're getting a very strong set of feelings and themes and images. And
    you get to do the work. You get to put that stream together in your own
    head in a way that's meaningful.
YARI: I want to add on to that. In his poems I noticed that he always has
    images of a gun and Black Jesus and you know drugs and his
    grandmother that's really been bothering him. I'm hoping to [see] or
    [hear] a poem that he's already released that stress.

The confusion that Aleyva and Jennifer, both first-year Power Writers,
articulated provided a forum for trying to understand Ron's work. Jennifer
shared her strategy of "picturing" what Ron was saying in order to help her
follow. Karina, a first-year Power Writer as well, was candid with Ron; she
believed he was going to lose his audience with the length and style of his
poetry. Ramon, one of the senior Power Writers who graduated mid-term,
suggested that his peers "look at the bigger picture" rather than try to catch
every word. Ramon also demonstrated that this process was going to take
time and a certain level of maturity. Everyone's comments provided Roland
with a forum to introduce the phrase *stream of consciousness.* Here, Roland provided the reader and the feeders with a context for the work while introducing a new idea. As all of this was taking place, Joe held everyone responsible
for collecting the words while also encouraging Roland to be as explicit as
possible in his definition.

Culturally relevant teaching, or teaching in context, are pedagogical
practices that most would agree are desirable, but knowing when and where
to enter as a teacher or how to use student work can be complicated. Here,
Roland used Ron's piece to introduce stream of consciousness. Roland was
vigilant about precision, and Joe always encouraged Roland to "break it
down" for the students. Beginning with a basic definition for *consciousness,*
Roland emphasized that students already had the prior knowledge they
needed to help them. Using the image of a stream, Roland was able to
evoke a sense of movement. Most important, Roland underscored that using this strategy was not necessarily a practice that would be used or valued
in school; however, it was still a valid way to express ideas. Amy's sug-
gestion that a stream-of-consciousness piece was "unedited" further pushed
Roland's feed and gave him another opportunity to affirm Ron's work. Note

that Roland's honesty with the Power Writers—"And it doesn't make sense the way we're taught to make sense"—puts the choice in the hands of the students. Finally, Roland built on Ramon's feed and Joe's metaphors, saying that Ron's style of writing was like a moving stream, and if you opened yourself to it, you would eventually hear its music and "feel it." This feeding of Ron's work was more than building vocabulary, constructing spellings, and generating definitions. Ron's feed became an effort to advance the relationships between teachers and peers. The care shown in Yari's final feed cannot be ignored either. Her final hope for her classmate was that he would be able to use the writing to heal himself.

"NATURE BOYS" AND BI-O-DI-VER-SI-TY

In order to collect words, students had to be willing to venture outside of their comfort zones. Over time, students realized that it was difficult to collect words in the same environment or with the same people. It was natural to develop a method of communication that did not require details or explanations. To counteract this tendency, Joe pushed to get as many Power Writers as possible to go on a camping trip away from the city. When the group returned, Joe challenged his "nature boys" to write reflective pieces about their trip, since he initially felt some resistance from the male students about going camping. Anthony, a recent Power Writing convert, was so excited about his post-camping piece that he brought a friend to class for its premiere. He announced, "It has no title."

As I close my eyes and embrace nature
I feel the wind and smell the scent that carries from the [inaudible]
I smell the different spices and pollens coming from different vegetation in
    the area
I hear a rush of water and the faint voices of my peers
I listen closely and I can hear different birds and animals in this biodiverse
    habitat
I feel nature's glow of crisp, cool air
I feel the sun and I just can't help bask in its warmth
I feel the embrace of my mother earth and enjoy the sensation she gives me
Out of all the excitement, I look across the lake and see the variety of
    browns and greens coming from the growing of leaves and I can't help
    but cheese
I smile and I was so glad I was starting to smile until I looked like the Kool-
    Aid man
I stood as nature sucked the breath out of my lungs
I am astonished

The sight was so compelling that it took me 30 seconds to realize I wasn't
    breathing
Even after I inhaled
The only word I even uttered was "Damn"

AMY: Me first? Wow, Anthony. What a change from the beginnings of your
    work. You are—you're really a master. You really are, and this is just
    another direction. Another beautiful one. Your language, your use of
    words, your rhythm, everything, it's just beautiful, and it makes me so
    happy that you're happy. You know? That you found this place to go
    that's about the different side of Anthony. You're a great writer.
ANTHONY: Thank you.

Amy picked up on Anthony's sense of happiness in his poem; she did not
let this get by and she wanted him to know that this new space advanced his
work. Manny, a student in one of Joe's classes and a very new Power Writer,
fed Anthony upon his request: "Okay, Anthony, after that trip we had, it's
like our whole vocabulary has changed. After that trip it's like we came back,
and we wasn't using the same words. It was like we stepped up to another
level. And you could tell in your writing."

Roland continuously nodded in affirmation while Manny fed Anthony
and also pointed at Manny as if to convey to the class, "He got it." Manny
believed this experience of traveling to a new place changed their vocabulary. All of us were visibly moved by Manny's feed; it confirmed Joe's fight
to get the students off campus and expose them to as much as he possibly
could beyond their borough:

ROLAND: Excellent mastery of vocabulary. Big, big switch.
JOE: I want to remind everybody, because I think Anthony did the best job
    of it, that our job when we're in these different situations is to fish for
    those words that we find in the world. And so I remember the kind of
    harsh lady and what she was doing with words. And I love the way you
    stepped to it because that was really important, you know? We played
    this little vocabulary game. And there were definitions on one card and
    the term on the other, and it was really quite wonderful to see my
    wordmasters see words they've never seen before but manipulate the
    definitions so cleverly that at some point what was lacking is we didn't
    have the scientific training but we certainly understood how to find
    definitions. And I like the bi-o-di-ver-si-ty. It was cool. I also like the
    symbol of the Kool-Aid.

Contextualizing Anthony's choice of words, Joe conveyed his sense of
pride in the Power Writers who played the vocabulary game during the trip.

In his signature style of feeding, Joe was able to move between feeding the entire group and specifically giving Anthony the feed he needed to take his writing to the next space, stressing his appreciation for the word *biodiversity* and Anthony's return home with the Kool-Aid man image. Heath's (1983) research of the literacy practices, and literacy events in particular, of two rural communities and Cushman's (1998) action research with inner-city residents navigating city and state social institutions showed that community members depended on each other to make sense of texts. Fishing for words and catching words were strategies that supported models of team teaching or collaborative teaching. Because of the multiple strategies and methods used to teach and understand words, the Power Writers benefited from working as a team with their peers and teachers.

CHAPTER SIX

Modern Blues Writers: Lived Experience as Literary Inspiration

"This poem is called 'Why do I write.'... I write because I had many unspoken words. ... I write not just because I'm a writer but because I am the words that I write."

—Jennifer

"Today is Friday, I get to relieve myself. Relieve myself of heartaches and headaches and all of the other emotions felt during the week. Putting my pen to my paper and letting my problems give way to a sense of relief to what was a tortuous week."

—Karina

"Why I am my writing. . . . Since I was younger I didn't know if I could do anything to escape the life that I went through but cry, to black out, to suppress. . . . Never a moment's rest, I walk down the streets past death and war, gun in hand in the form of a pen. I walk down tough roads of silent cries of those who were born into the game but can't get out. . . . Writing is an escape for me."

—Pearl

"This piece is called 'Because Joe wanted to know why.' . . . Why I write, why I write, why I write. To express and suppress certain images and certain feelings that cannot be understood by the people who understand me and why I am loud, vulgar and am who I am. Why I write, why I write, why I write. To break the chains that only remain so that I can look and seem to have shadows watching explain, 'He cannot survive in this world so he must remain in a domain that will do nothing but help him gain unaccomplished goals.'"

—Anthony

"If this classroom was my battlefield," Joe began as he looked around the table making eye contact with the Power Writers, "my tactical goal is for you to keep your dreams alive." Amy, Roland, and I were squeezing in wherever we could fit to make room for the students who were late. Every Power Writer was expected to compose a "Why I write piece" that would be a work in progress for as long as they were a part of the community. Encouraging students to hear the music in the writing, Joe explained, "For some of you, because we have the no-headphone rule at school and all of that nonsense, for some of you I want you to hear your music in your mind when you are writing and in your mind when you are reading. . . . I need you to find your song." Many of the Power Writers had taken Joe's music appreciation class and were familiar with his musical metaphors. Joe continued, "My tactical goal is for you to find your dreams. Do, quote unquote Malcolm, whatever is necessary to keep your dreams alive."

Making references to the blues should not be done haphazardly. It was ceremonial when Joe declared a member of the Power Writing family to be a blues singer or called someone's writing a "cosmic" or "modern" blues. In the context of Power Writing, the blues closely resembled Kelley's (2002) understanding of the blues as "true poetry" (p. 163). Hailing Paul Garon's *Blues and the Poetic Spirit* (1975/1996) as a road less traveled by blues scholars, Kelley asserts, "Unlike dozens of other scholars of the blues, Garon is less interested in what the blues may tell us about social reality than in comprehending desire" (p. 163). It was in the spirit of "comprehending desire" that Joe underscored the Power Writers' blues as a tool for dreaming strong and hard. In an era of accountability and testing in American public schools, the poet, narrator, and storyteller were expected to assume secondary roles in the hierarchy of traditional English classrooms. In Power Writing, these roles reclaimed their rightful place at the forefront of literacy learning.

The purpose of this chapter is to explore how the Power Writers redefined literacy to include mastering one's life story and providing rich details about everyday life, but first, I provide a framework for examining relationships between the blues, spoken word poetry, and the Power Writers. In order to analyze and reflect on Joe's references to the blues and the student writers in the Power Writing seminar, I draw from Woods's study of the blues as a "tradition of explanation" that is "embedded, necessary and reflective" (p. 25). Student writing was embedded; it was relevant, current, and grounded in the students' lives, and therefore, they were considered teachers as well as learners. Student writing was necessary; poetry was a place to release, grieve, and most important, overcome sadness. Student writing was reflective; the students looked back in order to create the world they desired.

In Woods's (1998) study of the emergence of blues during plantation power in the Mississippi Delta, he defines "blues epistemology" in the context of the lives of working-class African Americans in the rural south as "a system of explanation that informs their daily life, organizational activity, culture, religion and social movements" (p. 16). Woods posits that this tradition has other "branches, roots, and a trunk": "During the 1980s the blues were rediscovered by one generation of African Americans while another generation created rap which reaffirms the historic commitment to social and personal investigation, description, and criticism present in the blues" (p. 30).

Evoking the image of a family tree, Woods maintains that these two branches of truth-telling are the investigative practices of everyday people. Kelley (1994) argues that the blues is rap's "most significant ancestor," while others have suggested that rap was "configured" to confront issues such as pervasive violence "for which the blues is seemingly unsuited" (Garon, 1975; 1996, p. 192). The emergence of spoken word poetry has evolved from the roots of this same tree, providing youth with a hip hop ear an opportunity to reclaim poetry and use it to restore their faith in literacy learning. Students have the ability to "bring it," or use the grittiest lyrics and descriptions of the world around them, yet students can also "fall back," or be reflective, by using words that sneak up on listeners from behind. Spoken word poetry in youth culture is not entertainment; to borrow one of Joe's terms, this style of poetry is a "stickup." This "stickup," however, is not an attempted robbery. It is an attempt "to give you something."

Although the history of the blues originates with the African American working class in the rural south, Woods underscores that the foundations of this musical form are "essentially humanistic." One final, yet essential, link between the "blues bloc" in Woods's study and the Power Writers is the constant policing and attacks on independent thoughts that are sometimes imposed by public school culture. The need for a "free space," to borrow Kelley's term, for "comprehending desire" had to be carved out for the

Power Writers, much like secret societies of enslaved Africans from which the blues was born. Joe was committed to cocreating and sustaining a free space or a time in the day where high school students would learn how to use reading, writing, and speaking as tools for rewriting their life stories on their own terms. Power Writers characterized this class as the only space they had to write freely in both the physical and emotional sense. Manny compared poetry to "recess," while Dani confessed, "Poetry brought me back to school" after having lost interest. For others, such as Joel, who was completely isolated from his peers at the high school before joining the class, Power Writing was "the difference between life and death."

When a few of the Power Writers began to leave school on Fridays after attending Power Writing in the morning, Joe's intentions were questioned. Joe was adamant that students should return to their classes; however, he did not support administrative decisions to exclude students from poetry as a form of punishment. No one questioned why the students were committed to waking up early on Friday and Saturday mornings to write and to read poetry to each other for hours, yet were uninspired by what poet Ishmael Reed (2003) called "the limited vision of American missionary education that's driving blacks and Hispanics from the classroom" (p. xviii). This chapter looks specifically at the truth-telling tradition in the Power Writing classroom and the maintenance of a free space where high school students were considered vigilant and trustworthy witnesses to love, heartache, poverty, violence, and struggles for understanding.

PEARL'S PEARLS (OF WISDOM)

If ever there was a modern blues poet, it would be Pearl, whose haikus we read in Chapter 3. Pearl was the second oldest of five children. She and her three sisters were walking poetry; their clever names all began with the letter P. Her younger brother, Eric (the only sibling without a P name), was an honorary Power Writer. When I met Pearl, she had already written a 400-plus-page novel titled *I Have Truly Been Through It All,* based on her life experiences. Pearl would sing the blues in her poetry, send everyone into fits of hysteria, and look around with a beaming smile, mocking everyone by saying, "What's wrong with you?" In a class session that Joe dedicated to the "Bronx Diaspora," he asked Power Writers to address classically negative statements about Blacks and/or racism in their lives and communities. This assignment led to a series of Bronx-inspired poetry through which the students served as ethnographers for their communities. Pearl quickly responded to this assignment, naming the divisions that impacted everyone around the table:

My neighborhood is divided
Divided between Black and Spanish
We own our building but never in unity
We only tolerate each other
While I try to keep things that I do in my own mind
Race is just a word
Because I've been discriminated against by my own
Even though we're both Black
"She's lighter"
"She's better"
I'm all who I want to be
I don't hate
I don't want less
But I always want more
Black, West Indian, Cuban, Indian.
I'm everything.
I don't know.
Do collard greens go with rice and beans?
What do you think?
Yes, without knowing it
Our world we live by class systems
Where in certain parts there's predominately Spanish and Black
Or just Whites
Even though this occurs
My mind is not limited by shackles and chains
I am not better or worse than anyone else.
All my life I've never been accepted by my grandfather
Who doesn't speak English
He always told me I was darker than a brown paper bag
I'm the darkest in my family which goes from this (picking up something
     black)
All the way to this (picking up something white)
Racism will end with my cycle

Opening her poem with a neighborhood "divided," Pearl asserted that although her community "owns" the building, the sense of ownership is "never in unity." Pearl acknowledged that merely tolerating others kept the residents polarized. The irony in Pearl's poem was that the residents did not actually own their building, but they *did* own their prejudices against each other and themselves. Pearl's poem boldly confronted prejudice within families and, specifically, perceptions of lighter skin being "better." Autobiographical in nature, Pearl's poem reflected the discrimination she encountered as "the darkest" in her family, in which there were Black, West Indian,

Cuban, and Indian presences. For Pearl, racism surpassed Black and White or even Black and "Spanish" binaries because she had been discriminated against by her "own." Referencing a novel read by many UHHS students, *Do Platanos Go Wit' Collard Greens?* (Lamb, 1994), which is a story about a relationship between a Dominican woman and an African American man, Pearl discussed what was often left unspoken among her peers. Pearl's reference to "Spanish" people was commonplace around the Power Writing table. The term *Spanish* in this context did not mean people from Spain; instead, it referred to Spanish-speaking people who came primarily from Puerto Rico and the Dominican Republic. Being "Spanish" was a safe way to avoid being grouped with Blacks by using the Spanish language as a barrier, in spite of the fact that many people outside of the Bronx (and maybe within) could not distinguish who was "Black," "Dominican," "Puerto Rican," or "West Indian" around the Power Writing table. What began as an autobiographical piece about intra-racism in her family and neighborhood evolved into a social critique of the segregation Pearl experienced in the Bronx. Pearl set a precedent for truth-telling among her peers. She also saw herself as a blues singer. During our interview she made her own connections to blues traditions:

> MAISHA: How would you say that participating in the class has helped you with your writing, reading, and also speaking?
>
> PEARL: When I first got [to Power Writing], I was real quiet. The group strengthened me. I was real weak and uncertain of myself. But the poetry group helped me open up. They did not sugarcoat anything for me. Like when I first got there, I was a Blues singer. They told me that my words were strong and could rock you, Joe would say, and drop you. I went [from] the blues soft-spoken to the blues outspoken, like about domestic violence, and I became that woman. I took other people's lives, and I started to do my own life and to speak. I've always had a knack to speak publicly. The most nervous part is walking out onstage, but once you get there, then it feels like home.

Tracing the evolution of her own voice, Pearl distinguished between the soft-spoken and the outspoken blues. Pearl's statement returned to an earlier point made in the book, that student poetry often began with "I," "me," and "my." Over time, students learned to link their narratives to larger social implications. Assuming other voices, Pearl used her poetry to tell stories and sometimes cautionary tales about things that happened around the way. Pearl's style of truth-telling inspired her peers; in the next part of this chapter I examine how Pearl's peers built on this style of truth-telling to critically examine their neighborhoods.

DAILY ROUTINES, OR A BLUES FOR THE BOOGIE DOWN

Child of the Dark: The Diary of Carolina Maria de Jesus (1963) documents the monotonous nature of De Jesus' daily routine in her Brazilian *favela*. De Jesus rises each morning to collect scraps of paper in the hope of exchanging the paper for money to feed her children. What sets De Jesus' life apart from her neighbors, who also feel the daily pangs of hunger and poverty, is her ability to record her daily ritual in a diary when most of her neighbors are illiterate. In spite of its repetitive nature, De Jesus' book captivates readers with the almost rhythmic retelling of her daily routine. Power Writer Anthony followed De Jesus' truth-telling tradition (see also his poetry in Chapter 5). I noticed that either I was shrinking or Anthony was growing every week. Easily six feet tall, Anthony daily dodged basketball enthusiasts who insisted that the tall, young African American man must play ball. Anthony did not keep hoop dreams tucked under his pillow; he did, however, keep his book of seeds, or journal, near. Like De Jesus, Anthony narrated a story of "Shiquan and Sharise," who fall in love in the "land of the Bronx" only to find themselves in a mundane routine of public lives, arguments, abuse, and crime. For Anthony, or "Ant" as Joe called him, the story of Shiquan and Sharise was embedded in his simple yet telling title, "Daily Routine":

> An incipient relationship
> Shiquan an' Sharise
> Both very much in love
> Both very much confused
> Both very predictable
> Both born in a public hospital
> Both brought home on public transportation
> Raised in public housing
> Dropped out of public schools
> And now on public aid
> Now they live in a land of grim hysteria
> The land called the Bronx
> They both work in a place where they are daily patronized
> And don't even realize it
> They come home to arguments
> Mental and physical abuse
> They've been robbed 7 times
> Been to jail twice as many times as they were robbed
> Combined, they were shot 3 times and shot at 11
> They have 2 children that are forced to eat mayonnaise sandwiches
> And their beverage of choice is tap water with sugar
> At least with the odd color of the water

The children can pretend they're drinking tea
They must fight with rats and roaches
Or who gets to eat the moldy Western Beef bread
Shariffe and Narika could have a decent meal
If mommy and daddy didn't blow their salary,
Whose figures make the pay seem like an allowance,
On their daily fix
Young Shariffe is HIV-positive
But without insurance he can't get the right health care
So what are mommy and daddy supposed to do?
They don't know and they don't care
So they lay their children down to dream
Because these events have become a daily routine

Anthony marked the finality in Shiquan and Sharise's life by using past-tense verbs such as *born, brought, raised,* and *dropped* to define the couple's fate. Anthony also made an important social commentary about impoverished lives being public, beginning with hospitals, transportation, housing, and eventually schools and public assistance in a "land of grim hysteria." Portraying the Bronx as a land forced listeners to feel the isolation that those who inhabit this "land" may feel from the rest of the world. Anthony's details, like the blues, have a poetic spirit that was jolted by the mathematics of Shiquan and Sharise's existence. Playing with numbers as much as he played with words, Anthony introduced his readers to a cacophony of victimizing and victimization that touches the lives of the two children who come from Shiquan and Sharise's union.

Lives filled with mayonnaise sandwiches, sugar water, and inadequate health care were easily confirmed by the Power Writers, who had similar stories to tell. I was reminded of Adrian Nicole LeBlanc's *Random Family: Love, Drugs, Trouble and Coming of Age in the Bronx* (2003). LeBlanc spent over 10 years documenting the lives of Jessica and Coco, which were intertwined with drugs, sexual, and physical abuse and imprisonment (both mental and physical). In her author's note, LeBlanc responds to Coco's neighbors, family, and friends, who wanted to know why LeBlanc spent so much time following Coco when "Plenty of girls is worse off," by noting, "Certainly, I have found this to be true. The hardships of these young people and their families are not unusual in their neighborhoods. Neither are their gifts" (p. 406). Like LeBlanc, I became weary as I realized that stories of hardship seemed "routine" in student writing. However, I also know that these young people had a wealth of gifts. Anthony's gift was his ability to transform Shiquan and Sharise's "daily routine" into a sense of possibility at the end of his poem when he gently redirected the focus to the children; after all, it would be their dreams that provided the only conceivable exit from the daily routine.

Anthony also created music out of the mundane, transforming an otherwise prosaic narrative into something that caught everyone's attention. Here, Anthony gave the children the power to dream:

> ANTHONY: I heard Pearl, and that's when I started paying attention. . . . I was like a street kid. . . . I thought poetry was roses are red, violets are blue, and then I heard Pearl reading a piece about her mother . . . and then I heard Ramon and he was a rapper too . . . after that it was just over. It was like I was made for it . . .
>
> MAISHA: What is it about that style . . . about spoken word?
>
> ANTHONY: This is the reason I like spoken word a whole lot better than rapping. As a rapper you have to say what other people feel in order for people to like you. In spoken word you can be yourself and spit something you were feeling at that time. As long as you feel it, everyone else will feel it.

Writing about the Bronx was contagious after the Bronx Diaspora assignment. Everyone wanted to describe their borough from their own perspective. When I first heard Robbin read her piece "The Ghetto," she clicked her long acrylic nails together, creating a mnemonic device that secured a rhythm for each line of her poem. Robbin was one of five children, and Joe had taught two of her brothers. When Robbin had attendance problems, fellow Power Writers confronted her during the read and feed process and urged her to be as smart in class as she was in her poetry. Admitting that she had the ability to "catch attitude," Robbin emanated familial love for the Power Writers. On long Saturdays at Roland's, Robbin would put on music and force everyone to take a dancing break when the atmosphere felt too heavy. To this day, Robbin is the only person I know who could get Joe to show off a few dance moves. Robbin's brevity was telling; her ghetto was a place of cycles and open wounds that were never given time to heal: "My poem is called 'The Ghetto.'"

> While kids carry guns and baby girls have baby boys who have baby girls
> Who follow the grandmother's footsteps
> I think, why?
> While mothers have babies and telling their babies to watch their babies
> Yet telling us we're not grown yet
> With late night dates and early morning booty calls
> This is what I call the ghetto
> The ghetto is indescribable to those who have never lived there
> Where kids carry guns and baby girls have baby boys who have baby girls
> Who follow their grandmother's footsteps
> The path continues

Unlike Anthony's poem, which delivered a sense of possibility through the dreams of the children, Robbin's refrain—"While kids carry guns and baby girls have baby boys who have baby girls who follow the grandmother's footsteps"—painted an image of a never-ending cycle with little, if any, hope of escape. Robbin named the irony of parents making older children babysit younger siblings in spite of the fact that the older children were constantly reminded that they were not yet adults. Robbin chose "The Ghetto" to read at the second "Rebel Voices" public reading. During rehearsal, Joe fed Robbin: "It's a serious indictment of the world and the way we know it. Your tone in this piece has to be really hard and strong, okay? Really hard and strong. I want that poem done really hard and strong. These are terrible truths."

Students were trustworthy witnesses in Joe's eyes. His description of Robbin's poem as a "serious indictment of the world and the way we know it" validated her witnessing. Concluding his feed with "these are terrible truths," Joe acknowledged Robbin's intolerance for such conditions. Robbin's poem was also important because students across this country (and sadly, adults, too) use the term *ghetto* to describe anything perceived as low-class and as a signifier for race. The power of Robbin's poem is that she takes readers and listeners to a real place that is "indescribable to those who have never lived there," yet in a few lines she manages to deliver a powerful portrayal of hopelessness. I asked Robbin to explicate her poem during our interview:

ROBBIN: Basically if you notice there's always a story of a shoot-out in the Bronx or in the ghetto where minorities are mostly at where they call the ghetto. They put us down so much that we turn against each other. When we start shooting each other and girls go out and they think guys are the only ones that love them 'cause they parents are not getting along so they think the only way to feel love is they have to go have sex with a guy, end up pregnant, don't know what to do, and later on down the line it happens. It's a chain reaction.

MAISHA: Do you think the ghetto is a physical place or a mental place?

ROBBIN: Mental. Mental.

MAISHA: Talk to me about why it's mental.

ROBBIN: Because we don't live in such a bad neighborhood. It's the people. What makes our buildings any different than anybody else's building? Nothing. It's just the way you think. "Oh, I live on this side of town, there's more gum on the sidewalks than in Manhattan so this is the ghetto." No, it's not. Our staircases may not be all that, but we're still living in an apartment, we still have a roof over our heads. Food. Clothes on our back. It's a mental thing. They think, "Yeah they call us ghetto because we go to public schools." No, because a lot of people in Manhattan go to public schools.

Robbin believed the ghetto existed in the mind. She did not think that "more gum on the sidewalks" or staircases that were not "all that" were enough to cause one to think of oneself as poor. Robbin implied that Manhattan was the measuring stick for all New York City boroughs. This was not unusual, and Joe addressed this later in class. I asked Robbin to talk about her refrain, which made up most of the poem:

> MAISHA: Tell me about the line "Baby girls having baby boys having baby girls . . . "
> ROBBIN: It's like saying a girl will have a baby boy and she will have to raise him up. But she's a teenager so she's young, and she doesn't have that right parental vision to raise her son the right way. So he'll later on down the line go get another girl—get a girl pregnant and they're young parents then their baby girl [is] going to be on the same thing. Most kids who have teenage parents are going to do the same thing and end up teenage parents themselves. And it's a chain I've noticed throughout the years. I've noticed this with most of my friends.

Robbin emphasized that the ghetto was a mental space; however, she described a "chain reaction" of young women getting pregnant as a substitute for love. Robbin, much like Anthony, depicted prosaic lives. Robbin's explanation bore a startling resemblance to the opening pages of LeBlanc's *Random Family,* where "Grandmothers pushed strollers. Young mothers leaned on strollers," as if they had become props (p. 3). The use of refrains became a technique that Power Writers learned from each other. The refrains or choruses provided their poems with a musical quality. Eli's blues for the Boogie Down (a nickname for the Bronx) used this technique as well:

> Drugs invaded our culture
> And our raiders are being invaded
> I seek spirit because I cannot see sanity in any other way in today's world
> Fake solutions to fake problems
> I try to stay awake
> And my mother's living and dying wish
> Let her children stay humane
> So while I consume the air around me
> I see with my eyes what others said to me
> About the demise of our culture
> I consume air but know what it's like
> To consume the ashes to ashes, the ashes to ashes
> The dust to dust
> From the bodies of our people and those who have fallen behind
> To those who are empty shells of masks and lust

They choked me, they've weeped within me
They desire my mind for they have lost theirs
Their bodies lay out like streets made of concrete stairs
In the ashtrays we sometimes call the Boogie Down
Boogie Down
My throat sores of pain while men lash out at women
And women lash out at women and children
Women and children
We sink down the boat and lash out at women and children first
Listen to the Merengue and Salsa Blues
The Bachata and Cumbia Blues
The Conga Blues
While I lash out in bruises to the women's blues
Who gives a fuck if we outnumber you
And you, and you
When you're raped into fucking sorrow
Is there a tomorrow, a tomorrow, a tomorrow?
Bruised blue like the tears that eventually come tomorrow
May I live long enough to see the next day where I cry awake
Still sane. Still sane.
I don't ask for your fucked up sympathy
I ask for life as it's created like one big constructed symphony
This is my ode
And this is your ode
If you're the cause of this
May your children rebel from your foolishness I say
Lost out of your mind but in time inside
Look within you and you will see within you what's within me
I seek spirit because I cannot see sanity in any other way in today's world
Fake solutions to fake problems
I try to stay awake
And my mother's living and dying wish
Let her children stay humane
So while I consume the air around me
I see with my eyes what others said to me
About the demise of our culture
And I consume the air
But know what it's like
Know what it's like
Know what it's like

Eli traced how drugs transformed human beings into "empty shells."
As this drug invasion festered and the men began to take out their frustra-
tions on women, causing a chain reaction between women and children,

somehow music continued to play. Eli masterfully wove musical traditions from the Dominican Republic, Colombia, Cuba, Puerto Rico, and Africa together, while acknowledging that all of these types of music—merengue, salsa, bachata, and cumbia—have their own blues qualities, just like their listeners. Bachata, now a popular guitar-based music form in the Dominican Republic, went unrecognized by the mainstream because it was music from "*la gente baja*" or low-class people (Hernandez, 1995, p. xv). Cumbia, Colombian folk-dance music, was also affiliated with vulgarity, or "Black coastal." Eli's comparison of the Bronx to ashtrays and the consistent references to ashes and dust conjured emotions of a place and its people left behind. While people are lashing out at each other and the music is playing, Eli holds fast to his sanity in an attempt to honor his mother's "living and dying wish" for her children to protect their humanity in spite of their environment.

As Eli was reading his piece, Arline was busily finishing her poem. It was not at all unusual for students to write while others were reading, especially if they heard something that triggered an idea for their own work. I observed similar practices at spoken word poetry open mic venues. Poets would pull out their journals while someone else was in the middle of sharing work. This practice was not considered rude; it was in some ways a compliment because it showed that writers were inspired by each other. In her own way, Arline was listening to Eli, processing his words while simultaneously building on the ideas of her classmates: "This poem is called 'As Tears Escape My Eyes.'"

Tears escape my eyes as I see the fate of this world
Thinking about how much I love my ghetto girls and boys
I take a girl turn and twirl in her young innocence that doesn't exist
Her adult mind is something that we cannot fix
I look at her overdeveloped body
Big ass and lovely hair
Look in her eyes and see the child who's not even there
The sex and booty popping songs
Her dancing along to the song in the club where she doesn't belong
Tears escape my eyes and I wonder why I cry
And I see the boy
He's like a hungry lion trapped in a cage
He's 17 but he's had a gun since back in the day
The ghetto life. The ghetto life is what I am
The Bronx, the Boogie Down Bronx.
It's dirty streets
It's traffic
The people
I love it

The city where I grew up
As tears escape my eyes, I wonder why I cry
I cry for the mothers who have to bury their child and live alone
As tears escape my eyes, now I don't wonder why I cry.

Arline set up her poem to address the issues that young girls and boys in her community grapple with separately. For young girls, it was often their "overdeveloped" bodies that betrayed them, as well as the hypersexualization in the media and music that undermined their innocence. For young boys, it was the pervasive violence and the sense of entrapment. For the mothers, it was the fear of losing their children to any of these elements. Arline was also conflicted because she loved the people and the streets that had raised her but did not love the way young people were often forced to bypass their childhood. Joe fed Arline:

> I guess, Arline, what I'm most happy with is how you conduct your writing business in this house. You are able to use really concise language and present the vernacular and the idiolect of the street–I hadn't heard anybody talk about the Boogie Down in a long time. [A few students were talking and Joe addressed them, "Y'all going to roll over me?"] When I first came up here to work in the Bronx and I heard the expression "The Boogie Down" I didn't really quite understand it . . . you know, being from New York City, there's only one New York City and that's Manhattan. [Laughter] When I come out here I feel like I'm visiting South Dakota. [Laughter] But at the same time, by virtue of being here in the Bronx every day for about 5 years, the speed of it continues to shock me. How fast we're living and how fast we're dying. You're getting to be a compelling painter of image . . .

Referring to the Boogie Down, a nickname used for the Bronx and also part of the name of a pioneering hip hop group called "Boogie Down Productions," or BDP, Joe admitted that he did not know about the students' neighborhoods when he began his teaching journey. Students found his reference to South Dakota amusing, but like Robbin, Joe understood that Manhattan was the borough primarily associated with New York City. As Joe learned more about his students' lives through their writing, he expressed his concern for the pace of young people's lives. Living and dying fast would never be acceptable to Joe and he never wanted students to accept hardship as a "daily routine." Joe fed Arline and her development as a writer. Joe named Arline's power as a code-switcher and applauded her marriage between "concise language" and the "idiolect of the street." Arline served multiple audiences with her work: She could reach her peers, who would be familiar with some of her images, and she could also reach people who did not have the same point of reference. Referring to Arline as a "compelling painter of image," Joe affirmed his faith in his students as trustworthy witnesses to their communities.

Being a "compelling painter of image," which I would argue was an appropriate feed for all of these poems, links Power Writing traditions with the personal and social investigations, as well as elements of critique found in Blues poetry. For Joe this exercise in truth-telling, which he also acknowledged as "indictments" of urban America, was a strategy to help students name the factors they believed stifled individual and collective growth and development. However, witnessing and naming these social conditions was not the sole purpose for this work; the writing was a way to consciously forge pathways around potential pitfalls.

CHAPTER SEVEN

"We See Ourselves as Travelers": Building Literate Identities

Interviewing Joe was a never-ending journey that took place on the 4, 6, and A trains; during long walks through Bronx neighborhoods he referred to as "Gunsmoke"; tours of Harlem's Striver's Row; the Lower East Side; and whenever or wherever we could make the time. One Friday morning, Joe and I sat outside the classroom, while the Power Writers were using their morning writing time to work in their journals. During this part of our interview, Joe transported me back to his humble life growing up in New York in the 1950s. Joe's mother was an artist. I could picture this determined young woman, organizing reading circles at the kitchen table, regulating television viewing, and making her sons fetch "the little red wagon" on Saturdays for trips to "Sal's" (the Salvation Army) to

purchase secondhand books. "She really did not send us to school to learn," Joe explained, "she sent us to school to rehearse what we learned at home. . . . I had an adversarial attitude toward school."

Suddenly, Arline and Amanda appeared with journals and pens in hand, complaining, "It's too noisy in there." Power Writers were expected to write for 20 minutes on Friday mornings, while Joe, Amy, Roland, and I finalized plans for Saturday trips and took care of outstanding business. However, spring had sprung, and students had other things on their minds besides writing. Joe went into the room a couple of times to ask everyone to calm down in his signature low voice. However, when three more students walked by to find quieter spaces to write, Joe called everyone back to the room and let the Power Writers know how disappointed he was in their lack of commitment on this particular morning. Joe was visibly frustrated, and his voice was uncharacteristically shaky as he said, "I come in the room, close my eyes. Joel, Eli, Manny, and Anthony. It's the truth. No literate men." It was very still and silent. I knew how much Joe wanted his students to understand why literacy was the core of everything he taught; he knew from his own life that his ability to read, write, and think critically on some level "saved" him. Joe wanted to create the same sense of intimacy around literate practices for the Power Writers that his mother had provided for him and his brothers. Joe wanted his students to know that in spite of poverty and lack of resources, which his own family had experienced, the ability to read, write, and speak with great confidence was not only obtainable but imperative. Some students looked somber and lowered their heads, but others never looked away from Joe's eyes as he continued to address the glaring disparity between young men and women in the Power Writing class: "Thirty girls. Five boys." There it was. The elephant in the room had been named. Where were our young men? Two of them, Ramon and Alberto, graduated mid-semester and were on their way to college with full scholarships but not without struggle. "What do I see in the fellas? An opportunity to escape the higher mathematics of America. Your 'commitment numbers.' That's what I see you escaping."

In a poem that pays tribute to the late jazz drummer Art Blakey, Kamau Daáood uses Blakey's drumsticks as a metaphor for passing wisdom from one generation to the next. Countless trumpet players, saxophonists, pianists, bassists, and other musicians converged on The Jazz Messengers, Blakey's rotating collective of musicians, which was widely hailed as a jazz institution or "finishing school." Daáood (1997) underscores Blakey's commitment to teaching and learning with young musicians in the opening line of his poem, "I want to give Art Blakey's drumsticks to some child without a father . . ."

Daáood's poem is a call to the youth to listen to the old ones, who can "make them friends of wisdom," but I also read it as a challenge to the elders to make their lives, experiences, and wisdom available to the "children of asphalt." I consider Joe to be an Art Blakey of literacy; he mentored young writers and practiced his craft by their sides. Joe introduced the "old head" tradition in inner-city communities to the Power Writers (Anderson, 1990). "Old heads," according to Anderson's ethnography of an inner-city neighborhood, were older men and women who socialized young people with wisdom extracted from lived experiences. Anderson argues that the role of the old head was diminished by drugs and violence in impoverished neighborhoods. Duneier (1999) further explores the role of the old head in an extraordinary ethnography of book and magazine vendors on the sidewalks in New York City's Greenwich Village. Hakim, an African American book vendor in Duneier's study, is more than a bookseller with a table on the sidewalk; he holds discussions and debates and guides an intergenerational and crossgenerational group of men through a journey of literature. Duneier posits that in Hakim's "old head role," he is able to tell the young people when he is disappointed in them for not taking care of business and to "give advice based on the wisdom of experience or learning" (p. 38). Elsewhere, I examined intergenerational relationships between "elders" and newer poets at spoken word poetry open mic events (Fisher, 2003a; 2003b; 2004; 2006a). I argue that spoken word poetry communities have restored the role of the "old head"; elders in these communities consider it their responsibility to help newer writers see themselves as part of a literacy continuum.

Similarly, Joe considered the task of fostering a love for literacy among urban youth to be part of the responsibility of literacy educators. In Chapter 2, when Roland introduced Joe, he declared that if the school system had "10 Joes," it would be improved. There is a temptation to believe that only Joe can do what Joe did with this group of students. However, I would argue that his strategies are accessible and his philosophical underpinnings, which are interwoven in this book, are rooted in a respect and love for humanity that must accompany teaching in urban public high schools. Therefore, the purpose of this chapter is twofold. First, this chapter is an invitation to educators to think about their role and responsibility in helping young people build literate identities. I examine the trajectory of one student, Manny, who was the last to join Power Writing during the 2003–2004 academic year. Joe, Amy, Roland, and I agreed that in a short amount of time, Manny embraced the Power Writing process. I would also add that Manny's trajectory illustrates a case of moving beyond what Joe frequently referred to in class as "ascribed lives," or limited expectations, for young people imposed by schools, communities, and sometimes the young people themselves. Joe, Amy, and Roland took advantage of the opportunity to reinforce the purpose of the Power Writing seminar as well as the values of the community using Manny's participation as a road map.

Second, this chapter aims to show how students in the Power Writing seminar began to view themselves as literate, capable human beings who rightfully belonged to a community of poets and writers. In order to move beyond what Joe frequently referred to as "ascribed lives," the Power Writers redefined literacy to include their words, voices, and faces around the table.

In addition to analyzing Manny's trajectory, I also draw on qualitative interview data from the Power Writers. Manny's interactions with teachers and peers as well as interview data from the other Power Writers will provide a focused review of the pedagogical methods presented in previous chapters and a foundation for the implications for schools and communities.

MANNY'S MANHOOD

Manny joined the Power Writers during the spring semester after a busy football season the previous fall. Manny was in Joe's writing class, and Joe appreciated the fact that Manny was the only male student who "confessed" that he had read more than one book "cover to cover" when most of his male peers were posturing and pretending not to care. Joe explained to the Power Writers that he picked Manny "out of the pond" in his writing class:

> I picked you out of the pond in my writing class. You were the only male student in both classes when I asked could you cite for me two books you've read—remember when we did the activity on the critical lens? And I said you need to be able to refer to two books in an authoritative manner. Tell me the author. Tell me the title. Tell me what meaning those books have in the context of the critical lens. . . . And Manny sat there with another young brotha' who told me one time "I ain't never read a book from cover to cover" and everyone had their hoodie on backward over their faces [laughter], and [Manny] said "Oh-Oh. Only two books? Whip Bip" [Joe motions as if he has two books in his hands and he is throwing them out on the table ever so confidently in an effort to mimic Manny]. And then one of your books was Shakespeare. So I said, "What? Let me see if we know what this is. I thought Shakespeare was a fishing rod" [laughter]. And I don't want you to fear the desire to be different, you understand me?

In addition to celebrating Manny's courage to participate in class when one of his peers was seemingly uninterested, Joe applauded Manny's "desire to be different." Joe underscored his hope that Manny would never come to fear this desire. I was always amazed by the way Joe integrated humor and wit in his feeding. Joe teasingly referred to students' hoodies (a hooded sweatshirt), worn "backward over their faces," and this exaggeration resonated with everyone around the table; students knew what he was referring to and so did I as a former classroom teacher. Like Joe, I also knew that the students with the "hoodies on backward over their faces" were still our responsibility. Part of Joe's pedagogical strategy was to encourage, maybe even coax, these students out of their costumes and to unearth their gifts. Manny was one of these students.

A self-professed athlete, Manny dreamed of playing professional football "for the big ones." Known for his signature soft, curly hair that spiraled into a well-maintained afro, Manny would sometimes surprise everyone with a cornrow design. Other times he would pick all of his hair out. At the end of the semester, he really gave us a shock and shaved off all his hair. Although his hairstyles changed, Manny remained a consistent Power Writer. He was dedicated to improving his writing. Born in a Spanish-speaking household, Manny explained to me, "with speech I speak mostly Spanish, and I talk fast so when I speak English my pronunciation is not all that." Manny's first poem questioned the meaning of manhood and addressed the pressures he felt as a young Dominican man to mask his sensitivity and vulnerability. With his head down, resting his chin on a cane, Manny introduced his poem "Who Am I?" in a muffled voice in front of 20 strangers and Joe:

> Am I still a man or still a little kid?
> Am I still that predictable little boy?
> Am I the kid or the man who feels pain when no one's there?
> But that don't matter
> Because I'm a man
> That's what I tell myself
> Am I just a kid most of the time?
> Am I a man all of the time?
> Could it be a man like me is confused and doesn't know whether to be a
>   man or still a little child?
> Is it okay to feel this way?
> Who am I?
> And is it okay to feel this way?

Framing most of the lines in his poem as questions, Manny walked a fine line between his youth and what he perceived as the expectations of what it meant to be a man. Briefly finding resolution in the line, "But that don't matter because I am a man," Manny quickly returned to his uncertainty: "That's what I tell myself." I can still feel the stillness in the room as the "very cool" Manny revealed another side of himself to his peers. Students could not take their eyes off Manny. Cat, still working on feeding her peers, fed Manny:

CAT: I likeded how he–
SEVERAL STUDENTS IN UNISON: *LIKED*.
CAT: I liked his way of thinking who he is. He's questioning himself and
    then trying to answer himself.

This was a breakthrough feed for Cat; she was finding the language to analyze reflective writing, and she saw that Manny was giving everyone a window into his mind. Cat specifically liked the way Manny was both questioning and answering himself. The feeding continued with Karina, who was sitting on a windowsill:

> I thought that his poem was good. He kind of let you know what he was thinking at times like he's still in battle with himself whether it be one thing or the other. I think your writing could have been better if you would have— you see how you like crunched down? If you were to stand up stronger, your words would project better. And if you write, Joe taught me this, if you write it the way you want to say it, it will be easier for you to read.

Karina began her feeding of Manny's poem with what she liked; she interpreted Manny's poem as a "battle with himself." After focusing on something positive about the content of the poem, Karina directed the rest of her feed to the actual reading of the poem, suggesting that Manny stand up "stronger" to help project his voice. Karina also thought that if Manny considered reorganizing the poem on paper the way he wanted to read it, a lesson she had learned from Joe, then Manny might have a smoother reading experience. Karina's feed accomplished a few things: Karina shared her reflection of Manny's writing and gave him specific feedback, she gave examples of how to make his writing and public reading stronger, and Karina demonstrated her understanding of Joe's suggestions to the class. Generally, students received two feeds per read; however, since Manny was new he received multiple feeds:

> YARI: I look forward to listening to more of your poems. I like what was in your mind, but like she said try to stand up taller and don't be shy.
> ROLAND: What everyone's noticed is that while you were reading, you were putting your chin on your cane over your head.
> MANNY: I was nervous.
> ROLAND: Right, of course it's a way to deal with your nervousness, and we all have nervousness. But that was a really good first reading and really insightful and sensitive.

Yari's feed was a way to welcome Manny to the group and to encourage more writing. In her own way, Yari comforted Manny about being shy. Roland picked up on this and attempted to contextualize Manny's understandable nervousness. Waiting for everyone to feed Manny, Joe used his feed to address Manny and the rest of the class:

> It's interesting that you seized the opportunity to write the poem, which I think everyone gave you the courage to do. For anyone who is new, seize the time in here, you hear me? If we ask you to write about yourself, no

one said it has to be an autobiography or a narrative. All we said was write about yourself. Manny, I have you in my writing class, and I hope you know why I invited you here. I think this is where you belong. I think this is your community. These are your peers. And I'm really looking forward to helping you become a really good poet and a really good writer. You get much respect. That's a good job.

In his feed, Joe revisited the first assignment every Power Writer had to complete, a "Who am I?" piece to introduce themselves to the class. Students could use any format they chose for their autobiographical piece. What I think was most important about Joe's feed is that, rather than critiquing the poem, he focused on embracing Manny at a vulnerable moment. Joe modeled to the rest of the Power Writers that Manny was in his rightful place when he said, "These are your peers." Joe also alluded to his own responsibility in the process to help Manny improve as a poet and writer. To be sure, Joe's gesture signaled to Manny that not only was this a process that he was going to be a part of, but that he looked forward to helping Manny.

To end his feed with "You get much respect" was a powerful way to close this round of read and feed; the role of respect should not be underestimated. In an effort to deconstruct the way respect has become a form of social capital in inner-city neighborhoods, Anderson (1999) asserts, "When students become convinced that they cannot receive their props from teachers and staff, they turn elsewhere, typically to the street, encouraging others to follow their lead" (p. 96). Joe was acutely aware that one of the most important things that he or any other teacher could say to a student, especially a male student of color, was "Much respect." I believe that establishing this relationship around literacy is foundational; once respect is established, teachers and students expand the teaching and learning possibilities.

Manny's second reading took place approximately two weeks after his inaugural poem, and he introduced his poem by saying, "You guys are always going to have the question who am I talking to? I am talking to my little brother. I'm talking to him."

Sometimes I think what to do
Is my life going to be like theirs?
All my life I held back watching people die
For what? For nothing.
It's like God's holding me back by a thin string
I have dreams in other words nightmares
I wake up in the middle of the night
Scared
Gun in my hand
Drugs in my pocket

And I run
I have dreams. Yeah, I have real dreams of becoming
A great man, a great father, a great husband, a great brother and a strong,
    smart man
Everyday I feel like I'm one step closer to becoming the man my father *was*
And I don't want that
I want to be my own man
I'm sick and I'm tired of people telling me of what should I be, what should
    I do and where should I go
I want to be my own man
I'm gonna be my own man
You know why? Because I don't need you or anybody else
But do I?
I just don't want to be like that
Selling drugs, stealing, killing
But no, that's just not me
Some people say I have the smarts and I have the character
But I don't need to put you through this
Remember those dreams we had?
Of getting out of the hood, going to college, playing football
Some day playing with the big ones
And after that
Starting new dreams
But that don't matter no more
Because 'til then
God is still holding me back by a thin string.

Framed as an open letter to his younger brother, "Thin String" took
themes from Manny's first poem and explored them in greater detail. Again,
Manny confronted his fear of becoming the stereotype that people in his
school community and neighborhood sometimes expected him to fulfill.
This fear was so strong that it manifested itself in a dream/nightmare of
waking up in the middle of the night "Scared/Gun in my hand/Drugs in
my pocket." I was arrested by the way Manny portrayed his fear; there was
no recollection of where the gun and drugs came from, yet they were there,
implicating him in criminal activity. Using the imagery of a "thin string,"
Manny reminded his younger brother that the slightest misstep for either
of them could result in missing out on "getting out of the hood, going to
college, playing football." These missteps could also result in senseless and
untimely deaths, or, as Manny explained, "All my life I held back watching
people die. For what? For nothing." Manny's father, a hard-working man
and protective guardian, urged his sons to do well in school and would not
let Manny work until he graduated. According to Manny, his father did not

want him to enjoy making money more than going to school at that point in his life. Manny wanted to be "a great man, a great father, a great husband, a great brother" and "a strong, smart man" like his father became in his efforts to be a model for his sons. Ultimately, Manny believed the only thing that separated a lifestyle infested by drugs, guns, and death from becoming a good man was "thin string" held by a higher power. Amy fed his work:

> How many times have you been to class? Four? Five? Your honesty—you are using words that are extremely powerful. You're painting a picture of your life for all of us. You are giving yourself over to this process really in an open way. And because of that in just a short time that your work has grown tremendously. And I was just thinking as I was working on this book that I need your work. And you need to be included because you are definitely in the circle and you've taken this art form seriously. Thank you for being that open to us.

Once again, the strategy in feeding was to embrace Manny and emphasize the power of process. Amy welcomed Manny by urging him to submit work for the "Rebel Voices from the Heights Anthology" she had graciously volunteered to edit. Part of "giving yourself over to this process" was the commitment to be open. Amy also used the feeding tool for emphasizing Manny's rightful place in the Power Writing community; she wanted copies of his work to include in the anthology in spite of the fact that he had joined the group late in the academic year. Amy's voice was yet another affirmation of Manny's potential to take his writing as far as he allowed himself to venture. Here, Amy insisted that it was the Power Writing community that was fortunate to have Manny as a part of the circle. The power of multiple feeds from different people cannot be overlooked, either. Joe fed Manny after Amy:

> I judge people by their actions, not by what comes out of their mouth, so when I see you at school *schooling* and when you come into this circle you are writing about your life in a for-real manner—my response to you is not a criticism of your work, it's an acknowledgement of my respect for what you are doing. It's highly respectful work. We're glad you're here. . . . I hope you take tremendous advantage of it.

When Joe made a public acknowledgment that being "at school *schooling*" and writing "in a for-real manner" were inextricably linked, he sent a message to the Power Writing community that the commitment they demonstrated in their poetry had to be visible in school. In other words, students had to be citizens of the larger school community, and not just Power Writing. Building a foundation of respect was still a work in progress; this time, however, Joe alerted Manny to his hope that Manny would maximize his time in the class. When Joe changed voices and spoke on behalf of the Power Writing community, he modeled how to be a citizen in class and how to show respect for the work of others. How do students learn how to interact with each other if teachers do not model various approaches? I believe students are watching, waiting, and measuring teachers' words carefully at every level. When we are impatient, they learn to be impatient, but when we exhibit respect, they begin to emulate this essential value. By investing in students' economies of expression, English and language arts teachers have a unique opportunity to help students shape their future lives. Books, poetry, music, and films have transformed people's lives and defined movements—and all of these began with writing. Teachers must exercise patience as they help students evolve into the writers they want to become, and sometimes teachers have to carry this vision for students until they are able to carry it for themselves.

FROM A "KNUCKLE MASTER" TO A "WORD MASTER"

On the last official day of Power Writing during the 2003–2004 school year, Manny decided to recite his poem "End of Days." This poem was a return to Manny's first reading. Contemplating how his life and words would be perceived by others in his absence, Manny continued to ask himself reflective questions about his impact on others. Like many of his peers, Manny was concerned about whether his life—and, consequently, his writing—would carry a legacy. Would he be just another Dominican kid from the block, or would people actually care about his life?

> When the end of days come
> I will just be remembered as a little kid
> When the end of days come
> My ideas will be loathed by the rest of mankind
> When the end of days come
> Life will be life
> And nightmares will come to life to destroy everything caused by them
> When the end of days come
> All mind body and soul will be surrendered
> My poetry may be forgotten but I will be remembered

Joe chose to feed Manny for his final piece of the school year:

> JOE: Two pieces right away. In this house, we see ourselves as travelers. And
> for you to go from "My name is Manny and I can't write" to somebody

who thinks about the world in such a complex way, in such a serious way that (pause). . . . Something I was talking to Anthony about the other day, I claim you, I will always claim you. You mine. You are developing your mind, your desire to learn about the world. Those are your strengths. You used to be a boxer, and you used to be a knuckle master, and now you can master the word if that's what you want. It shows. . . . So for me it's tremendous progression in terms of your work. You have to read it over and over and bring it back to us. It's a really interesting poem, well-developed with *wordsmanship*. I want to encourage you to keep writing. It's really good.

MANNY: Thank you.

Reminding Manny of his proclamation, "My name is Manny and I can't write," which he made some three months earlier, Joe painted a picture of the Power Writers as travelers. As Joe guided the class in following the map of Manny's trajectory, he stopped along the way to crown him: "I claim you, I will always claim you. You mine." Translated from Bronxonics, this meant: "Not only are you mine today, but you are always mine, and you can come back home any time." For a teacher to "claim" a student is a sacred act. To return to an earlier point I made, I believe that an English language arts teacher in the 21st century has to be more than an expert in his or her content area; he or she must also be a healer, a practitioner of the craft, and a guide for students as they learn how to create their own literate identities. When Joe told Manny, "You are developing your mind, your desire to learn about the world," with the rest of the Power Writers bearing witness, he communicated that there was a relationship between literacy learning and developing one's full humanity. In other words, in addition to practicing the skills associated with reading, writing, and speaking, students first had to have a desire to increase their ways of knowing, ways of being, and ways of understanding. Without developing the desire to learn, students would be trapped. The Power Writers needed the ability to push through "ascribed lives" of being young people of color in one of the poorest areas in our country, a complicated road to navigate. Educators cannot ignore the fact that schools cannot be changed without confronting deplorable conditions in the students' communities (see Berliner, 2005). For the students to desire better living conditions, better schools, and better lives was the first stop on the journey, but there were many more. On this leg of the journey, it was essential for Manny, and his male peers in particular, to resist the pressure to become a "boxer" or a "knuckle master." To borrow Anderson's (1999) observations of inner-city neighborhoods, "verbal prowess" continued to have status in establishing one's identity around the way; however, physical displays of assertion still ruled the streets (p. 68).

The physical display of assertion, according to Anderson, is much quicker and, in some ways, easier to accomplish. The literate display—a road less traveled—would indeed take more time. In this "final" feed of the year, Joe gave Manny and his peers as much wisdom as he could before he set them free into the blazing New York summer. He also reminded them that as Jedis of words, Power Writers had some ongoing assignments: read, read, read, continue to collect words, and develop *wordsmanship*.

HEARING STUDENTS' MUSIC: IMPLICATIONS FOR SCHOOLS AND COMMUNITIES

What do I mean by "building literate identities," and why is this practice important for educators in urban school contexts? I believe it is every student's right to be given an opportunity to be a critical reader, a purposeful writer, and a confident speaker. Here, I do not draw lines in the sand separating the written and spoken word because the student poets used both mediums as they began to define themselves as writers. For the Power Writers, building literate identities began with crafting stories or "truths" using their own sense of style and rhythm. Like Joe, teachers have the ability to invite and welcome these individual and shared truths. Dyson (2005) summarizes this best in her examination of spoken word poetry in oral/written debates: "If you listen, you can craft in writing what you've heard others say and thereby give voice to your own responsive truth" (p. 154). In the Power Writing context, once students realized that they had the respect and encouragement of their teachers, they believed their words and ideas were valuable and worthy of being committed to paper. Students did not have to worry about being "correct" in the early phases of their work. For years, most of the students in Power Writing only remembered being "wrong," or, as Manny noted, being "used to thinking my opinions don't matter." Holding student work up as worthy of attention, even when it still needs improvement, is an important step in the process of students building literate identities. For many of the Power Writers, this step encouraged the students to take more risks with their writing over time.

Another important part of the journey of helping students build literate identities includes making them aware of the contributions their people have made to literacy and the literary arts. Elsewhere I argue that many young people and their teachers are unaware of the legacies of literacy of people of color (Fisher, 2004). For example, McHenry and Heath (1994) posit that many ethnic groups are assigned "cultural logos," such as being naturally "oral" as opposed to "literate." These cultural logos brand various ethnic groups, creating limitations about who may or may not be called a writer or a poet. One of the ways Joe combated these cultural logos as an educator was to try to provide links between novice poets and writers in his class and the literary activism of people of color. In the opening chapter, I introduced Joe's poem that historicized the Nuyorican Poet's Café and the Lower East Side Community. Joe took students to these landmarks to emphasize that people of color helped create and sustain literary institutions that met their needs as writers and poets. Scholars such as King (2006) argue that students have a right to access their "Heritage Knowledge." In other words, students of color should have opportunities to become "literate in [their] own heritage." Although King situates Heritage Knowledge in the experiences of students of African descent, other diverse students in American public schools also share the experience of having their people's contributions to literacy omitted from the English language arts curriculum. Educators have to become literate in these histories with their students; the journey and discovery can happen jointly. All students deserve to know what contributions their communities have made to language, poetry, prose, and song. English and language arts teachers also have to guide students to see where they fit into the literacy continuum and encourage them to extend their work in ways that are relevant to their lives.

"Poetry Is About Us": Spoken Word Poetry and Language Arts

In one of my questions to students, I asked why a class like Power Writing should be available to high school students. I wanted to know what students thought was most important about Power Writing—the way it was organized and how it was taught—that differed from a traditional English class. I also asked students to consider critics who challenged its relevance and importance in a testing-centered climate. Students mentioned values such as having "no boundaries," being "free," and not being "judged" within the Power Writing seminar; however, they also talked about how the class focused on their needs and desires. I was humbled by Amanda's brevity: "Poetry is about us. In English class the reading and curriculum is about them. The school's work. I don't like that at all." If students believe that the curriculum is solely "the school's work," then how can educators expect students to become engaged learners? Amanda's appeal is a reminder of how essential it is to create a curriculum for and with students that confronts issues that are relevant and timely and provide a mirror in which students can see themselves, their families, their communities, and, most important, their futures.

Like Amanda, Anthony had similar concerns about "regular" English classes: "In regular English classes they give you poetry. . . . when you are someone just getting introduced, you don't know what they are talking about, but when I heard spoken word . . . I got hooked." Anthony's response reflects the way "regular" English classes do not give students an opportunity to discover poets and writers outside the canon, which isolates the learner from the material. The reification of certain poets and authors excludes countless artists (maybe even some who are right there in our classrooms). Contrasting the poetry "they give you" in English class with spoken word poetry, Anthony said he became "hooked" on the type of poetry he could understand. It is possible that Amanda and Anthony's concerns tell us something about beginning with what students will recognize and understand, and then building on that knowledge.

As part of her passion for Power Writing, Arline also cited Joe's writing challenges and topics, which allowed her and her peers to explore issues of race, class, and identity:

> I don't want to read about a fictional character submerged in the sea. I like biographies. In poetry class it's like, "I want you to write about this." We don't get to learn until afterward. How do you say it? [Joe] gives us a challenge, and we get excited, then we read it out loud, and then he feeds us. I think it's a matter of choice that really helps us.

Arline believed that her time was best spent reading nonfiction; she had a lot of questions about people and places that she found she could begin to answer through reading and exploring. Arline also valued learning in context; she was learning but she did not realize it until "afterward." What Arline and her peers were really discovering was that learning did not have to be painful.

Choice was also important to students; they were convinced that the "school's work" and their own writing were in two separate worlds, and Power Writing was the only place where they merged the two. However, students also learned how to connect what they learned in Power Writing with some of the institutional expectations about which they did not have any choice. For example, Karina talked about how she was able to use her knowledge in poetry for the writing portions of standardized tests:

> In school it's such structured writing, and I don't believe everything should be structured. In Power Writing we still write about topics with our own twist. . . . Being able to write whatever you feel on command helps with my structured writing. With the ability of me being able to think of something so fast, it's much easier for me to do, so I'm not stuck anymore as far as tests go. When I get a piece of writing that I've never read before, I can make my structured writing my own. It just feels like I'm writing another piece about my own topic.

By applying the values and practices in Power Writing to other writing situations, Karina learned how to be less fearful of responding to writing prompts that she was seeing for the first time. She also referenced the writing challenges that Joe, Amy, and Roland would often give to the class; students did not always know ahead of time what they would be writing about and often had to compose a response in the form of a poem in 20–30 minutes in class. Many writing challenges emerged from topics Joe heard around the Power Writing table. Creating a curriculum based on student ideas requires careful listening. Joe not only kept a journal for his poetry, but he also kept detailed notes while students were talking so he could keep track of the ideas that were being generated in class.

Students needed to know that there was another possible curriculum—one that included their voices. Poets and scholars such as Miguel Algarín, Bob Holman, Ishmael Reed, Zoë Anglesey, and many others have anthologized communities of poets whose ideas and life experiences have been undervalued. African American poet and scholar Ishmael Reed (2003) noted, "I had read excellent white writers for years during my education, but it wasn't until I read the young James Baldwin while working at a Buffalo library that I felt I had a shot" (p. xxviii). The value of having "a shot" in the Power Writing community cannot be overemphasized. Joel, one of the original Power Writers, helped me understand the power of having a shot through his journey:

> Joe has never called an idea of ours stupid. I finally had a reason to care about this work. Now it's you go to high school, you take the Power Writing course, you get into college, and you change the world. Now I feel like with these hands and my mind I can change the world. I can write something down and be taken seriously.

Joel calls attention to a critical part of this journey; students began to care about writing and to develop a skill set that allowed their ideas to be taken seriously by an outside audience.

"Come Share My Words": Spoken Word Poetry and Positive Peer Pressure

Students in this writing community contradicted monolithic depictions of minority students as anti-intellectual or punitive to peers who demonstrate care for school and learning. In her study of urban students' academic communities, Walker (2006) asserts that high-achieving Black and Latino students are often assumed to be isolated from their peers. Walker further argues that these assumptions potentially "negate or undervalue" supportive peer influences (p. 51). Although Walker's study focuses on math peer groups, the Power Writers also demonstrated that urban students' desire to be successful does not have to be in conflict with their need to feel accepted by peers.

Positive peer influence was critical to students. Syesha noted, "If my peers see me in the hallways they tell me to go to class." Not only did Power Writers read their poems to each other before and after class to get ideas about content and delivery, but they also asked each other for help with spelling and proofreading. Manny shared with me that he frequently went to Pearl so she could correct his spelling errors. What I found equally compelling was how the class helped students get to know their peers without depending on convenient stereotypes to assess one another's worth, as Arline explained:

> Like for instance, you see somebody in the hallway, and it's another face in the crowd. A lot of people [in class] I would never hang out with on a daily basis, but once you get to know them they are pretty cool. Everybody here has their own clique; you would never expect by looking at certain people what kind of things they are into. I'm like "I write, do you write?"

I think it's important to note that students struggled with the same issues teacher struggle with, such as making value judgments about young people based on outside appearances and stereotypes. For Arline, "another face in the crowd" was transformed into a potential writer. I believe Arline's experience was at the core of why Power Writing was one of the most diverse classes where students were not worried about who was "Black" or who was "Dominican," who had their hat on backward or who wore braids. The "Bronx Diaspora" challenge discussed in Chapter 6 was a way for students to think about the shared realities and responsibilities around the table as opposed to finger-wagging at particular groups. The Power Writers wanted to know, "Do you write?" They also learned how to take pride in their own literate identities and became comfortable earning a reputation as writers and readers. Pearl and I had many conversations about self-esteem and young women. Pearl saw many of her female peers learning that the only way to "get the guy" was by having "the hair," "the skin," and "the figure," but not "the mind":

> Many people come to me and ask me for help. I might not be the one they want to be with, but they know who's going to make it because every time they see me I'm writing. Every time they see me, I'm reading. They know I'm focused. Maybe I don't skip school to hang out with guys because that's not me. [The other girls] may have the body, but they don't have the mind.

Pearl influenced many of her peers and motivated them to take their writing seriously. Anthony confessed to me, "I heard Pearl, and that's when I started paying attention." Anthony explained that his early poetry style focused on women and sex, but Pearl's work and discipline inspired him to write about other topics. Most important, Pearl learned that she could take pride in being a young woman with the "mind." In fact, Power Writers learned a lot about their personal development. When Karina and I sat down together, she summed up many of the themes that emerged from her peers: "Everyone has a different story to tell. Everyone is from the craziest rage to the beautiful flower. Everyone respects each other's space, and sometimes you can be invited into that space. Come share my words."

Reciprocity was at the core of this practice. Students learned how to be honest with each other and not just to compliment their friends' poetry. Karina learned how to listen and honor the range between "the craziest rage" and "the beautiful flower." Arline shared similar words: "It's a partnership. Equal equal. They help me. I help them. It's all good." Earlier, in Chapter 5, I alluded to Joe's commitment not to colonize his students. Again, I cannot confirm whether the students fully understood this part of Joe's mission, but the students did learn that their lives and their cultures were not monolithic.

"Be as Smart in the World as You Are in Poetry": Spoken Word Poetry in the Classroom and Beyond

Earlier I underscored that literacy and being literate, in the context of the Power Writing classroom, were not mysterious forces. Joe tried to make the process of being or becoming literate as visible as possible. In Power Writing, students had an opportunity to try literacy on, so to speak, to find the right fit. Most important, students did not only see the finished product when it came to literacy. They became tailors learning the inside seams, forgotten threads, and all the imperfections of the process. Power Writers focused on what was referred to as the "three literacies"–reading, writing and speaking–in class. Although it was not discussed in class this way, I would also add that listening was a fourth type of literacy that was critical in Power Writing. Spoken word poetry allowed students to work on mastering all of these practices. The reality was that the class was making up for lost time. Many of the students came in as struggling writers and readers. Once they started writing, using the medium of poetry, however, they did not want to stop. The Power Writers could talk about literacy and they had their own interpretations of Joe's desire for them "to be literate in as many ways as possible":

> Don't only be smart in your writing, but have the same open mind in reality. Don't mumble, or when you go to a place like a political event, you won't speak like . . . "Yeah that's what's up" or "What's up, my nigga." And also how to act, too. When I read, I stand up straight, and I spit out my gum. [It means] to be as smart in the world as you are in poetry.

Cat's description of being literate, above, echoed Nieto's (2000) description of "*educado*" in Latino communities. *Educado,* or being educated, according to Nieto, also includes "being polite, respectful and obedient" (p. 159). Cat saw potential in using poetry to practice ways of being in the world. Standing up straight, removing her gum, and being "smart" in the world outside of poetry were tangible practices Cat believed she could put to use anywhere. Once again, the read and feed process discussed in Chapter 3, the video camera, and the microphones were all representatives of a much larger audience that Joe wanted the Power Writers to be able to address. For some Power Writers, being literate in as many ways as possible was about defying negative stereotypes about people of color and forcing other to get to know them for their fluidity with language, as Pearl emphasized:

> Joe's telling us that we have the tools and to use them, have knowledge, try to get to soak up as much as you can, so when you walk into a room, you cannot be talked down upon. Use the tools as much as you can because when you leave here you're not going to find anything like this. No one is going to teach you to look up in a way you never have before and take you to places. I think this is the only place you can get that.

Power Writers seemed most compelled by the image of walking confidently into a room of strangers and being able to engage anyone in that room in thoughtful, articulate conversation. It was not a coincidence that the class had an open-door policy for visitors, or that public readings included colleagues from education, nonprofit, and artist circles; this was a way for students to learn how to communicate widely. This tool, according to Pearl, would help students "look up in a way you never have before." It was very important to the students that people not write or talk "over them." Unfortunately, the common narrative among the Power Writers said that school had been a place where words and language were used to create distance between people and to reify status and power. In contrast, the Power Writing class employed language to foster a sense of intimacy with literate practices. Poetry clubs and other forms of writing are all too often considered extracurricular, relegated to afterschool clubs or special programming one night during the school year. Many nonprofit organizations have committed themselves to promoting student writing through the arts and are frequently being asked by schools to conduct workshops and seminars (see Appendix C).

This study has demonstrated the different ways that young poets learned to establish writing discipline, articulate themselves, explore new vocabulary, and use writing as a form of healing. All of these goals should be part of the English and language arts curriculum. Power Writing, however, should not have been the only place where students could "get that," as Pearl duly noted. Pearl and her peers wanted and deserved to know why people who looked like them and lived where they lived were not always at the table in particular situations; they wanted to know how you got to sit at the table and be comfortable without changing the nature of your being completely. Scholars have emphasized how minority students often associate academic success with "acting White"; however, in all fairness to the students, I believe educational researchers will also have to examine how schools reinforce this mythology through tracking, segregation, and substandard learning environments. Students were ecstatic by the prospect of surprising those who had consistently doubted their abilities. Manny dramatized the process of pulling out his paper or his essay as a way to overwhelm nonbelievers:

> To me it's like Joe always tells me, I'm too quiet, and I let people stereotype me because of the way I dress and the way I look. Joe always says that people are always going to try to put you down for your skin color, the way you talk. But once you come out with your writing, with your paper, your essay and you smack them in the face with your literacy, it's going to be crazy!

Rather than waiting for an invitation to sit down at the table, the Power Writers were learning how to select their own seats. For the concepts of literacy and being literate to take on these multiple meanings in the context of this class did not minimize basic skills. Instead, students saw a purpose for the work they were doing and became invested in the process. Ultimately, being literate in all literacy's forms was a lantern illuminating new pathways and ways of traveling, or, as Amanda explained, "open[ing] your mind to a different style of writing, words, and expressions." Arline compared being literate to an awakening of new worlds outside of one's block, neighborhood, and borough: "From what I hear, it's not only the Bronx. It's not only New York City. It's not only the ghetto and the projects. It's not just slang and Bronxonics. You have to open your mind."

In the opening narrative of this chapter, Joe passionately conveyed to the Power Writers his belief that literacy was an opportunity to escape "the higher mathematics of America." In other words, becoming a Jedi of words was a way for students of color to live lives outside the dismaying statistics of failure, poverty, and, as Robbin noted in Chapter 6, "mental imprisonment." Joe's Jedis of words experienced everything from "I can't write" to "with these hands . . . I can write something down and be taken seriously." Exposure was essential to helping students see beyond ascribed lives. Students learned how to listen in particular ways to discover a language that would allow them to convey their feelings about things they witnessed and heard. Being "literate in as many ways possible" included behaviors or actions that reflected a sense of belonging in this world, or being claimed. Like

Jordan's (2000) memories of a poet's childhood, being chosen was an act of beauty. Young people are yearning to be chosen and to be claimed. Teachers must recognize this yearning and help young people develop the tools to transform this yearning into words and actions that chart the future they desire and deserve.

Afterword

Just a brief reminder, the do-rags are not the minds; the backward hats are not the hearts. What a difficult task it is to teach literacy in 21st-century America. As a people, we have not reified our core values of liberty, fraternity, equality, and justice. These failures return like Marley's ghost to haunt us. Our internal contradictions imperil us all. Do we, as Dewey argued a century ago, bring the world to our students, or do we accept and abet the ascribed and oppressive circumstances that constrain our pupils' perceptions of literacy, its structures, and their functions? We remain a class society, and as such, our ideas, our worldview, and most important, our language are shaped by our class positions and the rigidity of still-prominent ethnic, racial, and economic barriers.

Ask yourself: Is your class a sanctuary, a temple of knowledge, an arena within which your students can learn the skills of critical thinking and contemplation, analysis and postulation, the science of the language and the exploration of the rich mother lodes of literature? Do we understand the complexity of modern English in America? Is this understanding manifest in defining the work that we do and the methodology of such work? Does society at this time really desire a literate citizenry, or do many of its structures depend upon an ascribed culture of silence, illiteracy, and political impotence?

Do we, do we, do we ever stop to ask how it was that we achieved literacy? Why it was important to do so? What circumstances made such effort and achievement possible? These are the real "how, now, brown cow" questions of transference, assimilation, and acculturation into the realms of the literate. The answers to these questions are the force of history in motion. Let us examine our class experiences—how information was acquired by our families and passed on to successive generations. Where did we acquire our ideas about information and knowledge?

When I think of the students with whom we have worked in Power Writing over the past 5 years, the first thing that comes to mind is the importance of encouraging young men and women to tell their own life stories and to model the skills that are the prerequisites to this most important endeavor. The manifest function of our writing circle is to have our students acquire the ability to examine the world, to analyze and speculate as to the order of things, to problem-solve and to articulate their perceptions through the medium of writing. We create a physical and ideational sanctuary where all voices are of equal value, where form and function serve only to build community and to make communication possible. The one cannot exist without the other.

Our students deserve and demand literacy and a safe space in which to acquire and rehearse the elaborate and complex convergence of the written and the spoken word. They all want to speak to and for the world, to reveal what is real to them, their triumphs and their sorrows. In short, they all wish to be heard, beyond the ascribed modalities of silence and violence.

The choice to use creative writing, specifically poetry, as the driving force behind the literacy project has very much to do with the conventional and fallacious perception of the role of poetry in our society as a secret doctrine, the esoteric of the elite. The poetry of the blues, of jazz, and of American popular music contradicts this assumption of literary exclusivity and serves to remind us of the elemental import of the spoken word. We are all Americans and what we speak is American English, as what we live are American lives. The work then becomes a process of redefining and refining our students' relationship to the language. Print is more than an encryption of the auditory form and thus requires a kind of cognitive mapping. We must identify a path for our students and a rationale for the arduous task at hand, the acquisition of literacy. English class will always be for me a call to arms.

–Joseph R. Ubiles

Student Information Chart, 2003–2004 Academic Year

STUDENT NAME	AGE	GRADE	ETHNIC BACKGROUND*	YEAR(S) IN POWER WRITING
Ron	19	First-year community college	African American	Second year
Ramon	18	Twelfth (Graduated mid-year)	Dominican	Third year
Alberto	18	Twelfth (Graduated mid-year)	Dominican	Third year
Eli	19	Twelfth	Colombian/ El Salvadorian	First year
Joel	18	Twelfth (Graduated mid-year)	Dominican	Third year
"Buddha"	19	Transferred to another school	Dominican	Second year
"Pink"	19	Twelfth	White/ Puerto Rican	Second year
Syesha	18	Twelfth	Puerto Rican	Second year
Manny	18	Eleventh	Black/Dominican	First year
Arline	17	Eleventh	Dominican	First year
Amanda	16	Eleventh	Dominican	First year

Kenya	18	Eleventh		First year
Pearl	17	Eleventh	Black/White/ Spanish/Indian/ West Indian/Cuban	Third year
Anthony	17	Eleventh	African American	First year
Dani	16	Eleventh	Belizian	Third year
Karina	16	Tenth	Puerto Rican	First year
Robbin	15	Tenth	Black	First year
Yari	17	Tenth	Dominican	First year
Maddie	15	Tenth	Dominican	First year
Kari	16	Tenth	Dominican	First year
Aleyva	16	Tenth	Puerto Rican/ Dominican	First year
Cat	15	Ninth	Dominican	First year
Jennifer	16	Ninth	Puerto Rican/Indian	First year
"Red"	16	Ninth	Puerto Rican	First year (Dropped in)

*As self-identified by the students.

Joe-isms

CODES/ ("JOE-ISMS")	STUDENT DEFINITION(S)	JOE'S EXPLANATIONS:
Literacy/ Being Literate	"Joe always says that people are always going to try to put you down for your skin color and the way you talk. But once you come out with your writing with your paper, your essay, and you smack them in the face with your literacy, it's going to be crazy!" (Manny)	"I read a lot of literary theory because I am profoundly conscious of the caste elements of language. And I am old enough to come from a generation where our parents told us language would be used against us, so get busy." "As long as we continue to produce legions of young men and women who cannot read, write and think independently, we are a subject people"
Jedi of words	"Learn every word and the history of the word." (Ron)	"We sharpen our language like we sharpen knives."
Singing	"I wrote something about my oldest brother and the first time I read it and Joe said it was beautiful but I need to sing it . . . he wants us to put emotion and flow with it." (Amanda)	"Do not deny the emotion in your work!"
Read and feed	"[Read and feed is] instrumental. We read our work. We put our whole self out there. We are expecting to get hurt, but instead of getting hurt, we are learning and you really get to polish your work." (Dani)	"You can really only do the pieces you believe in. Each of you has a piece that you truly believe in. If we are rehearsing, it is not to have pressure. It is to increase the level of beauty. I promise you it's going to be beautiful, but you have to practice."

Bronxonics	"It's not only the Bronx, it's not only New York City, it's not only the ghetto and the projects. . . . It's not just slang and Bronxonics. You have to open your mind. [Joe] gives us books to read and I have a list of books . . . and he says this will inspire you to write a different way." (Arline)	"It's our responsibility to teach [our students] the full breadth and scope of the language and to never be ashamed of proficiency. And at the same time to redefine that proficiency. . . . Bronxonics is to be real. To be aware that what we speak in each of our respective neighborhoods, at some level, is dialect and a worldview."
Catching words	"I write words down, and then I go home and look them up in the dictionary. I would play a game; flip the dictionary, find words, and write them down. I picked 13 words and used them in a poem." (Cat)	"This is a STICKUP! We're trying to give you something. I want you to collect words and ideas."
Telling the "truth"	"Some people may not like my work, but when I get on the stage, I don't care if you like me or not. I say what I have to say and get off the stage. The poetry group is my life." (Pearl)	"If this class is a battlefield, my tactical goal is for you to keep your dreams alive."

Resources for Educators

Blackout Arts Collective: www.blackoutartscollective.com
Atlanta: atlanta@blackoutartscollective.com
Boston: boston@blackoutartscollective.com
Washington, DC: dc@blackoutartscollective.com
Houston: houston@blackoutartscollective.com
New Haven: newhaven@blackoutartscollective.com
New Orleans: 504-339-3154; neworleans@blackoutartscollective.com
New York (National Office)
    266 West 37th Street
    New York, NY
    212-594-4482 Ext. 17
    newyork@blackoutartscollective.com

California Poets in the Schools
1333 Balboa St. #3
San Francisco, CA 94118
415-221-4201
www.cpits.org/

Early Stages
410 West 42nd Street, Suite 4E2
New York, NY 10036
917-699-0625
earlystages@earthlink.net
www.earlystages.org

The Expanding Canon: Teaching Multicultural Literature in High School
Workshop 8/Critical Pedagogy
with Abidun Oyewole and Lawson Fusao
www.learner.org/resources/series178

June Jordan's Poetry for the People
696 Barrows Hall
African American Studies Department
University of California
Berkeley, CA 94720
510-642-2743
http://poetryforthepeople.org/

Teachers & Writers Collaborative
520 Eighth Ave., Suite 2020
New York, NY 10018
212-691-6590 (phone)
212-675-0171 (fax)
info@twc.org
www.twc.org

To Be Heard: A Documentary About the Lives and Poetry of the Power Writers
www.tobeheard.org

Urban Word NYC
242 W. 27th Street, Suite 3B
(between 7th & 8th Aves.)
New York, NY 10001
212-352-3495
info@urbanwordnyc.org
www.urbanwordnyc.org

Youth Speaks
290 Division St., Suite 302
San Francisco, CA 94103
415-255-9035
www.youthspeaks.org

Youth Speaks Brave New Voices Program
(cities throughout the United States):
www.bravenewvoices.org

References

Algarín, M. (1994). The sidewalk of high art: Introduction. In M. Algarín & B. Holman (Eds.), *Aloud: Voices from the Nuyorican poets café* (pp. 3–28). New York: Henry Holt and Company.

Alim, H. S. (2005). Critical language awareness in the United States: Revisiting issues and revising pedagogies in a resegregated society. *Educational Researcher, 34*(7), 24–31.

Anderson, E. (1999). *Code of the street: Decency, violence and the moral life of the inner city.* New York: W.W. Norton & Company.

Anderson, E. (1990). *Street Wise: Race, class and change in an urban community.* Chicago: University of Chicago Press.

Ball, A. F. (1992). Cultural preference and the expository writing of African-American adolescents. *Written Communication, 9*(4), 501–532.

Baraka, A. (1996). Foreword. In A. Oyewole, U. B. Hassan, & K. Green (Eds.), *On a mission: Selected poems and a history of The Last Poets* (pp. xiii–xvii). New York: Henry Holt & Co.

Baugh, J. (2003). Linguistic profiling. In S. Makoni, G. Smitherman, A. F. Ball, & A. K. Spears (Eds.), *Black linguistics: Language, politics and society in Africa and the Americas* (pp. 155–168). London: Routledge.

Berliner, D. (2005). Our impoverished view of educational reform. A Presidential Invited speech presented at the annual meeting of the American Educational Researcher Association, Montreal. Retrieved from http://www.tcrecord.org/Content.asp?ContentID=12106

Christensen, L. (2000). *Reading, writing, and rising up: Teaching about social justice and the power of the written word.* Milwaukee, WI: Rethinking Schools.

Cushman, E. (1998). *The struggle and the tools: Oral and literate strategies in an inner city community.* New York: State University of New York Press.

Daáood, K. (1997). Art Blakey's drumsticks. *On Leimert Park* [CD]. Simi Valley, CA: Mama Foundation.

Dahl, R. (1947, 1952). *Matilda.* New York: Penguin Books.

De Jesus, C. M. (1963). *Child of the dark: The diary of Carolina Maria De Jesus.* New York: Mentor.

Duneier, M. (1999). *Sidewalk.* New York: Farrar, Straus and Giroux.

Dyson, A. H. (2005). Crafting "The humble prose of living": Rethinking oral/written relations in the echoes of spoken word. *English Education, 37*(2), 149–164.

Fecho, B. (2004). *"Is this English?" Race, language, and culture in the classroom.* New York: Teachers College Press.

Films for the Humanities and Sciences. (2004). *Do you speak American?* Princeton, NJ: A Films Media Group company.

Fisher, M. T. (2006a). Earning "dual degrees": Black bookstores as alternative knowledge spaces. *Anthropology and Education Quarterly, 37*(1), 83–99.

Fisher, M. T. (2006b). Building a literocracy: Diaspora literacy and heritage knowledge in participatory literacy communities. In A. Ball (Ed.), *With more deliberate speed: Achieving equity and excellence in education—Realizing the full potential of* Brown v. Board of Education [The 105th Yearbook of the National Society for the Study of Education Part 2] (pp. 361–381). Malden, MA: Blackwell.

Fisher, M. T. (2005a). Literocracy: Liberating language and creating possibilities. *English Education, 37*(2), 92–95.

Fisher, M. T. (2005b). From the coffee house to the school house: The promise and potential of spoken word poetry in school contexts. *English Education, 37*(2), 115–131.

Fisher, M T. (2004). "The song is unfinished": The new literate and literary. *Written Communication, 21*(3), 290–312.

Fisher, M. T. (2003a). Choosing literacy: African Diaspora Participatory Literacy Communities. Unpublished dissertation, University of California at Berkeley.

Fisher, M. T. (2003b). Open mics and open minds: Spoken word poetry in African Diaspora Participatory Literacy Communities. *Harvard Educational Review, 73*(3), 362–389.

Fishman, J., Lunsford, A., McGregor, B., & Otuteye, M. (2005). Performing writing, performing literacy. *College Composition and Communication, 57*(2), 224–252.

Freire, P. (1998). *Pedagogy of freedom: Ethics, democracy and civic courage.* Lanham, MD: Rowman & Littlefield Publishers.

Freire, P., & Macedo, D. (1987). *Literacy: Reading the word and the world.* South Hadley, MA: Bergin and Garvey.

Frey, D. (1994). *The last shot: City streets, basketball dreams.* New York: Simon and Schuster.

Garon, P. (1996). *Blues and the poetic spirit.* San Francisco: City Lights. (Originally published 1975)

Heath, S. B. (1983). *Ways with words.* Cambridge: Cambridge University Press.

Hernandez, D. P. (1995). *Bachata: A social history of a Dominican popular music.* Philadelphia: Temple University Press.

Herrera, J. F. (2000). *The upside down boy/El niño de cabeza.* San Francisco: Children's Book Press.

Jordan, J. (2000). *Soldier: A poet's childhood.* New York: Basic Civitas Books.

Jordan, J. (August 1988). "Nobody mean more to me than you and the future life of Willie Jordan." *Harvard Educational Review, 58*(3), 363–374.

Kelley, R.D.G. (2002). *Freedom dreams: The Black radical imagination.* Boston: Beacon.

King, J. E. (2006). "If justice is our objective": Diaspora literacy, heritage knowledge, and the praxis of critical studyin' for human freedom. In A. Ball (Ed.), *With more deliberate speed: Achieving equity and excellence in education—Realizing the full potential of* Brown v. Board of Education. The 105th Yearbook of the National Society for the Study of Education, Part 2. Malden, MA: Blackwell Publishing.

Kinloch, V. F. (2005a). Poetry, literacy and creativity: Fostering effective learning strategies in an urban classroom. *English Education, 37*(2), 96–114.

Kinloch, V. F. (2005b). Revisiting the promise of *Students' Right to Their Own Language:* Pedagogical strategies. *College Composition and Communication, 57*(1), 83–113.

Lamb, D. (1994). *Do platanos go wit' collard greens?* New York: I Write What I Like, Inc.

LeBlanc, A. N. (2003). *Random family: Love, drugs, trouble and coming of age in the Bronx.* New York: Scribner.

Lee, C. D. (2001). Is October Brown Chinese? A culturally modeling activity system for underachieving students. *American Educational Research Journal, 38*(1), 97–141.

Lee, C. D. (1995). A culturally based cognitive apprenticeship: Teaching African American high school students skills in literary interpretation. *Reading Research Quarterly, 30*(4), 608–630.

Lieber, C. M., & Poliner, R. A. (2004). *The advisory guide: Designing and implementing effective advisor programs in secondary schools.* Cambridge, MA: Educators for Social Responsibility.

McHenry, E., & Heath, S. B. (1994). The literate and the literary: African Americans as writers and readers–1830–1940. *Written Communication, 11*(4), 419–443.

Nieto, S. (2000). *Affirming diversity: The sociopolitical context of multicultural education.* New York: Longman.

Pink, S. (2001). *Doing visual ethnography.* London: Sage.

Reed, I. (Ed.). (2003). *From totems to hip-hop: A multicultural anthology of poetry across the Americas, 1900–2002.* New York: Thunder's Mouth Press.

Rickford, J. R., & Rickford, R. J. (2000). *Spoken soul: The story of Black English.* New York: Wiley.

Schultz, K. (2003). *Listening: A framework for teaching across differences.* New York: Teachers College Press.

Scribner, S., & Cole, M. (1981). Unpacking literacy. In M. F. Whiteman (Ed.), *Writing: The nature, development, and teaching of written communication* (pp. 71–87). Mahwah, NJ: Erlbaum.

Shabazz, J. (2005). *A time before crack.* New York: powerHouse Cultural Entertainment, Inc.

Shor, I. (1992). *Empowering education: Critical teaching for social change.* Chicago: University of Chicago Press.

Smitherman, G. (1999). CCCC and the "Students' Right to Their Own Language." In G. Smitherman, *Talkin that talk: Language, culture and education in African America* (pp. 375–399). London and New York: Routledge.

Street, B. V. (2005). Recent applications of new literacy studies in educational contexts. *Research in the Teaching of English, 39*(4), 417–423.

Street, B. V. (1993). Introduction: The new literacy studies. In B. V. Street (Ed.), *Cross cultural approaches to literacy* (pp. 1–21). New York: Cambridge University Press.

Street, B. V. (1984). *Literacy in theory and practice.* Cambridge: Cambridge University Press.

Torres-Guzmán, M. E. (2004). Language, culture and literacy in Puerto Rican communities. In B. Pérez (Ed.), *Sociocultural contexts of language and literacy* (pp. 111–135). Mahwah, NJ: Erlbaum.

Ubiles, J. (2004). To teach power writing. In A. Sultan (Ed.), *Rebel voices from the Heights* (pp. 18–19). New York: Early Stages Press.

Walker, E. (2006). Urban high school students' academic communities and their effects on mathematics success. *American Educational Research Journal, 43*(1), 43–73.

Woods, C. (1998). *Development arrested: The blues and plantation power in the Mississippi Delta.* London: Verso.

Index

About the Author

Maisha T. Fisher is an assistant professor in the Division of Educational Studies at Emory University. Her research examining the intersections of literacy and identity in school and in out-of-school settings has been published in *Harvard Educational Review, Written Communication, Anthropology and Education Quarterly,* and *English Education.*